A Study of 1 & 2 Kings

TRUSTWORTHY

OVERCOMING OUR GREATEST STRUGGLES TO TRUST GOD

LYSA TERKEURST

Lifeway Press®
Brentwood, Tennessee

Published by Lifeway Press® • ©2023 Lysa TerKeurst

No part of this book may be reproduced or transmitted in any form or by any means, electronic or mechanical, including photocopying and recording, or by any information storage or retrieval system, except as may be expressly permitted in writing by the publisher. Requests for permission should be addressed in writing to Lifeway Press®; 200 Powell Place, Suite 100, Brentwood, TN 37027-7707.

ISBN 978-1-0877-7874-7
Item 005841000
Dewey decimal classification: 234.2
Subject heading: FAITH / TRUST / KINGS AND RULERS

Unless otherwise noted all Scripture quotations are from The Holy Bible, English Standard Version® (ESV®), copyright © 2001 by Crossway, a publishing ministry of Good News Publishers. Used by permission. Scripture quotations marked NIV are from THE HOLY BIBLE, NEW INTERNATIONAL VERSION®, NIV® Copyright © 1973, 1978, 1984, 2011 by Biblica, Inc.® Used by permission. All rights reserved worldwide. Scripture quotations marked (KJV) are from the King James Version Bible. Scripture quotations marked CSB are been taken from the Christian Standard Bible®, Copyright © 2017 by Holman Bible Publishers. Used by permission. Christian Standard Bible•, and CSB® are federally registered trademarks of Holman Bible Publishers.

To order additional copies of this resource, write Lifeway Resources Customer Service; 200 Powell Place, Suite 100, Brentwood, TN 37027-7707; FAX order to 615.251.5933; call toll-free 800.458.2772; email orderentry@ lifeway.com; or order online at www.lifeway.com.

Printed in the United States of America

Lifeway Resources,
200 Powell Place, Suite 100, Brentwood, TN 37027-7707

Cover Design: Alison Fargason

Photos on pages 8, 35, and 70, courtesy of Steven Bussell @seventhstory.com.

CONTENTS

MEET THE AUTHOR

Lysa TerKeurst is passionate about God's Word. She spends hours each week studying with theological experts and has studied extensively in the Holy Land. She loves to make connections between the Old and New Testaments. Her deepest desire is to help others experience Jesus by unpacking Scripture in the most true and responsible ways that everyone can understand.

Lysa is the president of Proverbs 31 Ministries and a #1 *New York Times* best-selling author of *It's Not Supposed to Be This Way*, *Uninvited*, and twenty-one other books. But to those who know her best she's just a simple girl who holds fast to God's truth and speaks about hope in the midst of her own struggles. Lysa lives with her family in Charlotte, North Carolina.

Connect with her at LysaTerKeurst.com or on social media @LysaTerKeurst.

INTRODUCTION

I stood in front of the busted up walls amazed by all I never knew was behind them. Wires. Pipes. Support beams. Insulation. It all stood out now so very vulnerable and exposed. I ran my hand along the rough reality of renovation and thought how very similar my heart felt at the moment. The only difference was I knew my house would be put back together, better than ever.

I wasn't so sure about my heart.

With the house, I knew a basic time frame. I also knew enough about renovations to add a few months of buffer time to the end date. Regardless, I absolutely knew there would be a beginning to this project and there would be an ending to this project. I also knew the end result would be beautiful. And since I knew the basic time frame and how beautiful things would eventually be, the busting up part of the renovation didn't bother me. I was actually happy that demolition occurred.

The demolition was not a sign of irreparable problems. It was a sign of intentional progress. But I couldn't say the same about the busted up places of my heart. Not right now. Not yet.

When I stood and looked in the mirror, my demolished heart wasn't quite as easy to see as the walls in my house. The brokenness certainly revealed things, but they weren't as easy to identify as pipes and wires. They were strange threads of fear, anxiety, shock, trauma, and distrust.

Distrust. There it was. The biggest of all the issues that resided beneath my surface. The ripping open and exposing of my heart had certainly revealed something I needed to see but didn't dare want to admit.

About me. About God. And about my utter lack of trust in Him.

Now, don't get me wrong, I'm a Jesus girl through and through. I love studying His Word, doing the right and required things, following Him, and fulfilling my calling. Yes, yes, sign me up for all of that.

But when God starts to deviate from the plan I'm assuming my life should follow, I'm much more apt to want to tame God, not trust Him.

And then when a busting up of all that felt safe and secure happens without any assurance of a completion date and a vision of the exact good that will surely come from this—well, that's when I slide my raised hand down and I quit volunteering so eagerly to follow hard after God. That's when I kick into high gear resisting God's plans, making suggestions of how to do this whole thing better, and start pulling away from trusting God and pressing in to my ways, my timing, and my assumed better plan.

I demand the builder hand over the tools, and though I have *no clue* how to truly make things better, I start patching and covering and frantically fixating on a hodgepodge repair that will be disappointing at best, detrimental at worst.

I see this so clearly in my house renovations and have no desire at all to displace the master builder.

I just wish I could have this same clarity in my trust of God.

At the risk of exposing too much of my absolute flesh tendencies, I'm going to peel back a protective layer of my soul. I absolutely want to trust God. And I'm good with declaring my trust of Him. But declaring faith is not the same as walking out an absolute dependence on God to be God. That's where I want to build altars of my own solutions and run to fixing things my way rather than fixing my eyes on the Lord and actually trusting Him.

In both cases I'm worshiping. But worshiping my desires over worshiping God Himself is not an altar that honors God. Quite the opposite.

In biblical times, there were patterns around God's people building high places, which at first can seem like "something foolish those people did." But what I just described that I do—worship solutions and plans of my own making—makes this personal. It's not just an issue to study about them. It's a significant spiritual erosion that must be addressed in my soul—not one day but today.

But understand, addressing this isn't because God is disappointed in me. He's actually appointing this time for me to understand the depth of His love for me like never before.

That's why I can't think of two more perfect books of the Bible to dust off and dig into than 1 and 2 Kings. What appears from the outside looking in as ancient text about long-ago leaders with faith-faulty hearts isn't so far removed from addressing the exact issues I need to examine in my own life.

As I've dared to read these books from the vantage point of needing the truth treasures buried inside of them, I've been astonished at how much application there is for a girl who loves God but finds herself resisting Him in ways that are way more dangerous than I've ever cared to admit before.

And I wonder why I find myself so very exhausted and anxious and heavily burdened on the inside while singing and quoting verses about the abundant Christian life on the outside.

There is a disconnect somewhere between the faith I want and the one I'm living.

I know you feel it too. I've seen it in your tear-filled eyes, and I've heard it in your questions around the harder things to understand about God.

So, let's create a safe place to acknowledge our distrust and discover how God will give us relief for our places of unbelief. Together, we will find a more grounded faith, renovated hearts, and a strengthened trust in God like never before.

ABOUT THIS STUDY

In this study we will spend time with some people who may be familiar to you, but more than likely, we will meet a few royal men whom we previously didn't know all too well. As we study the lives of several Old Testament kings, we will learn together from their mistakes, misplaced affections, and successes.

We'll dive deep into the lives of a few kings from the pages of the Old Testament. A few things you will want to know:

- Your Bible study book comes with access to the videos that accompany this study. You'll find detailed information for how to stream the video teaching sessions on the card inserted in the back of this book. The first video session is an introduction to the series.
- Then, each week in your personal study time you will study one, or sometimes a few, kings from the Books of 1 and 2 Kings.
- In the video following your week of study, I'll unpack a little more about the kings you just studied that week.

This was an intentional format because I want you to study the stories of the kings for yourself and dig into Scripture on your own about each one before I give you my thoughts on the subject.

For the sake of clarity, I'm teaching from the English Standard Version in this study. If you're using another version of the Bible, it might be helpful to also look at the ESV on your computer or mobile device.

You will have five days of personal study each week.

During the study, we will be looking closely at the lives of several of the kings found in the Old Testament. We won't be covering every single king in depth. At the beginning of each session, you'll see a chart of all the kings with a little bit of background on the king we're studying next. This will help you to connect the kings in your mind and get an idea of the context each one is entering into. We've also provided a guide in the back of the book that will take you through the entire Books of 1 and 2 Kings if you'd like to know more and get the full story of the history of God's people.

My prayer for you in this study is that you will discover that God alone is worthy of our trust and worthy to rule our hearts. I'm praying that together we'll overcome our doubts about who He is so that we can rest in Him. I'm so grateful to be taking this journey with you.

TO ACCESS THE VIDEO TEACHING SESSIONS, USE THE INSTRUCTIONS IN THE BACK OF YOUR BIBLE STUDY BOOK.

WATCH VIDEO SESSION 1 AND RECORD YOUR NOTES BELOW.

Distrust

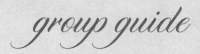

VIDEO GROUP DISCUSSION QUESTIONS

After watching the video, discuss the following questions in your group.

- In the video, Lysa said, "When God starts to deviate from the plan I'm assuming my life should follow, I'm much more apt to want to tame God, not trust Him." How does this speak to you?

- As we learn more about 1 and 2 Kings, remember, we're not just studying history but intentionally looking for how these books apply to us personally. Is there an area in your life where trusting God seems complicated?

- It's easy to declare that we trust God, but what does it really look like to walk out a life of faith?

- How would you explain the Israelites' distrust of the Lord when He did not fail them or betray them?

- How does our lack of patience add to our distrust of God and others?

- What will it take for us to have more trust in the Lord? How can we encourage one another in this?

To access the video teaching sessions, use the instructions in the back of your Bible study book.

11

Saul, David, and Solomon

TRUST IN HIM AT ALL TIMES, O PEOPLE; POUR OUT YOUR HEART BEFORE HIM; GOD IS A REFUGE FOR US. SELAH

PSALM 62:8

#TRUSTWORTHYSTUDY

WEEK 1
INTRODUCTION

First of all, can I admit something to you? The Books of 1 and 2 Kings have never been high on my list of priorities to study. It's not that I don't find the history of what happened to the Israelite people interesting. Quite the opposite actually. Since traveling to Israel many times to study, I'm more interested in their history than ever. I guess I've been hesitant because of six reasons. Maybe you can relate.

1. I've never been a king. I'll never be a king. So why would I want to examine the lives of kings?

2. And since these are ancient kings, even if they have life lessons to learn from, will those lessons apply to me in my life today?

3. These books of the Bible feel confusing. There are a lot of kings. There's an eventual split within the kingdom of Israel, which makes the number of kings even greater. There's a host of prophets that make the number of people involved even greater.

4. And let's be honest, I've never heard of many of these people, so it can feel a bit intimidating.

5. The repeated pattern of the disobedience of the kings can seriously get on my nerves and feel exhausting.

6. I need someone to lead me through this and help me make sense of all of this.

Here's the good news: I decided to jump knee-deep into this study and see if I could lead people through it. Do you know what I discovered? I'm completely fascinated by these books now. I've learned lessons I needed more than I ever realized. And I'm so very humbled by how much I not only relate to these kings but how much my heart needed to soak in the deeper human angst of learning how very trustworthy God is.

I do want to assure you—we're studying lessons from the Books of 1 and 2 Kings. But you'll notice we'll also be in some other books of the Bible that will help us get the greater historical context of these events.

You probably already noticed in the first video that we went all the way back to Genesis and talked about the importance of Deuteronomy 17 and other Scriptures throughout the Bible. You'll also notice cross-references to 1 and 2 Chronicles, which give us a different perspective of the events that take place in 1 and 2 Kings. We'll refer to various proverbs and psalms, too, that originated in the times of the kings or were written by some of these very kings. We'll even jump forward into the New Testament to see how passages in the Old Testament are crucially tied to the development of what takes place. Ultimately, the experiences of the Israelites being led by these imperfect human kings helps us see more clearly our need for the one true, perfect, and righteous King, Jesus.

I say all of this to help give you a bigger context for studying 1 and 2 Kings.

One last note to alleviate any confusion as you start Day 1. You'll see the verses we start with are from 1 Samuel (not 1 Kings). That's because the anointing of the first king happens before the Books of 1 and 2 Kings begin. And I'll be using the ESV (English Standard Version) of the Bible, unless otherwise noted.

King SAUL

Note: If you haven't read the Week 1 Introduction, please do so first.

On paper, everything seemed to make perfect sense. There was an opportunity I'd wanted for a long time. In my best estimation, this seemed to line up perfectly with my ministry, my calling, and my desires. The only problem was the deep-down knowing it wasn't my assignment. I'd asked God for this opportunity, but then I'd worked tirelessly behind the scenes to make sure I'd get it. This opportunity was the product of my trying really hard, not truly trusting God. And I felt the weight of all my hustle. I was anxious, exhausted, and weighed down by an emotion I couldn't quite understand—dread. It had felt so right. It had seemed like such a good fit. It made perfect sense when I'd said yes. But the closer the due date came for this opportunity, the more regret I felt. Instead of running in the freedom of being assured that God had called me to this so He'd definitely lead me through it, I felt like I was pushing a boulder uphill.

There is a weight to our every want.

And when God says no or not yet, it's often because He can see what the weight of this want will do to us. Make no mistake, we will eventually realize what our choices outside of God's will cost us.

Now, buckle your seatbelt; we're about to get into some theology. Don't get overwhelmed, just lean in and take from this what is helpful to you. My goal is to make something complex simple. When we say, "God's will," we are fully acknowledging God's "sovereign will," but we are dealing with "will of command" here.

When we talk about God's will, that phraseology is layered with meaning. There's an obvious mystery there that will never be fully understood by the human mind.

But for the sake of correctly defining what is meant by God's will in this study, consider the definitions below.

God's Sovereign Will—When we talk about God's sovereign will (Gen. 50:20; Matt. 11:25-26; Acts 2:23; Rom. 9:18-19; Eph. 1:11), we mean that, regardless of the situation or circumstance, God's sovereignty is supreme and human history is under His authority. In all honesty, some parts of God's sovereign will are a mystery to us. This is where we need to return to the character and nature of God. Because God is good, we can trust His sovereign will to be good (Rom. 8:28).[1]

Will of Command—When we talk about God's will of command (Matt. 7:21; Eph. 5:17; John 4:34), we are talking about God's precepts or commands He has made known to us primarily through His Word. Theologian Wayne Grudem is helpful in saying, "Because God's revealed will usually contains his commands or 'precepts' for our moral conduct, God's revealed will is sometimes also called God's will of precept or will of command. This revealed will of God is God's declared will concerning what we *should* do or what God *commands* us to do."[2]

God has expectations for how humanity, whom He created in His image, is to live and act. Yet, sadly, humanity is prone to wander, and this is the repetitive story we see throughout Scripture. However, even in the midst of our disobedience and wandering, God's sovereign will brings unity and authority to these events, making them subject to Him.

THERE IS A
WEIGHT TO
OUR EVERY
WANT.

Using the information and the Scriptures cited above, define "sovereign will" and "will of command" in your own words.

God's sovereign will provides a foundational security. But His will of command offers only possibility.

So how do we tie these two together? God is in control. But He doesn't control our choices. God has given responsibility to humans to choose Him, His way, and His best.

OUR OBEDIENCE TO GOD'S WILL OF COMMAND IS ACTUALLY AN INDICATION OF WHETHER OR NOT WE TRUST HIM.

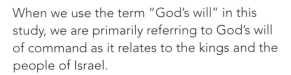

When we use the term "God's will" in this study, we are primarily referring to God's will of command as it relates to the kings and the people of Israel.

Like I said earlier, we will eventually realize what our choices outside of God's will cost us. And that moment of realization leads us right back to what God tried to tell us before we ever made those choices. There isn't ever a time when God has been wrong.

Not ever. And how gracious of God to be patient with us as we learn that lesson over and over. God is trustworthy. Our obedience to God's will of command is actually an indication of whether or not we trust Him.

Let's take a look at how the tension between obedience and trust played out with God's people and the first king to rule over them—Saul.

Saul certainly looked the part of a king. Read 1 Samuel 9:2 and record his external qualities. *handsome, very tall*

Consider 1 Samuel 10:17-19. What are they losing by rejecting God and choosing a human king? *protection, saving from disaster relationship w/ God who delivered them from slavery in Egypt.*

Read 1 Samuel 8:11 and compare it with 1 Samuel 11:5-8. As you read 1 Samuel 11:5-8, notice the anger within Saul that was greatly kindled and the severity of his reaction. How does 1 Samuel 11 fulfill what God said would happen in 1 Samuel 8?

Saul called an army to protect the people & he did take all the sons & lead them into battle.

God warned them that human kings would be harsh and would send them into battle.

Sometimes when we read examples in Scripture of God saying, "don't do this," we only hear that God is being so restrictive.

How might the example in the last question help you better understand other Scriptures where God is saying "no" as a protection woven into the restriction? Write a verse or example from the Bible that initially felt too restrictive, but you can now see as a protection.

eating the apple from the tree in Garden of Eden.

How could understanding this deepen your trust in God?

God can always be trustworthy.
His saying No is a protection against something bad for us.

We have to be careful of viewing God's restrictions in our lives as God being unfair or cruel, because this can lead us to question God's goodness. However, when our perspective changes and we see God's restrictions as evidence of His protection, we see God's goodness and care. This truth brings us to a realization that His restrictions are truly a grace given to us.

Read 1 Samuel 12:8-12 and fill in the chart below.

Circumstances that caused the people to cry out	Those whom God appointed as leader(s)	The results of their leadership
after entered Egypt, people cried to Lord for help	Moses + Aaron	brought your ancestors out of Egypt + settled them in this place
people were worshipping Baal - God gave the ppl to Philistines + King of Moab - they cried out	Jerub-Baal Barak Jephthah + Samuel	they delivered from enemies + lived in safety
they saw Nahash King of Ammonites + asked for King to protect them		

What did Samuel say was required of the people and king of Israel in 1 Samuel 12:14-15?

Fear the Lord + serve + obey him
Do not rebel his commands

Read 1 Samuel 12:16-19. What was the weight of the want of a king for the people of Israel?

God thunder + rained and they realized Samuel had direct connection w/ God since he asked for it.

Saul had just won a battle and been confirmed king (1 Sam. 11), which should have been a time of celebration. But the prophet Samuel saw something the people were slow to perceive: they exchanged God's best for the weight of their own choice.

Where have you exchanged God's best for something you wanted?

Sleep or tv/relaxation for doing something for others?

THEY EXCHANGED
GOD'S BEST FOR
THE WEIGHT
OF THEIR OWN
CHOICE.

As a result, in addition to obeying God, they would also be held accountable for the choices of a king they would not be able to control. When this king went astray, the people would suffer.

Read 1 Samuel 13:8-14. What was Saul afraid of, and how did this fear result in distrust of God? *Losing against another country— he did burnt offering to a false God.*

How did Saul take things into his own hands? What were the consequences of this choice? (See 1 Sam. 15:27-28.) *He tore Samuel's robe, and now the kingdom will be torn from him.*

Because of Saul's disobedience, God found another king who was better than Saul to lead His people. This king was a man after God's own heart (1 Sam. 13:14), and his throne would be established forever (2 Sam. 7:16).

King DAVID

Let's pick up where we left off yesterday. Right after Saul was rejected as king, God sent Samuel to anoint the next king. First Samuel 16 tells a story you may be familiar with. God told Samuel to go to Bethlehem to a man named Jesse. God had selected one of Jesse's sons to be the next king. Samuel went through the sons one by one looking for the one chosen by God.

Read 1 Samuel 16. In verse 7, what did God tell Samuel to look for (or not look for) in the next king? *Do NOT look @ appearance, height. Look @ ♡*

Finally, Samuel asked if there were any other sons, and Jesse told him about his youngest son tending sheep.

Sometimes, when we feel rejected by people, we feel like we've been overlooked by God as well. But this story is such a beautiful example: even though David was not chosen by his father to be brought in from the field, God ensured David didn't miss his assignment. When you've been chosen by God, even people's rejections will not override God's assignment.

How does the story of David being chosen by God for the assignment of king speak to you personally? *Trust in God's assignment for me*

Look at verses 14-23. What happened to Saul? *evil spirit tormented Saul. God's spirit left him. Saul appointed David to play lyre to relieve his torment. David gained Saul's trust & became Armor-Bearer*

Saul was still king at this point, even though David had been anointed as the next king. David was sent for because he could play the lyre to help calm Saul's spirit. David comforted King Saul and was allowed to stay in the court.

In 1 Samuel 17 we see that one day during a battle with the Philistines, David came to the front lines of the Israelite army to bring food to his brothers, who were fighting in battle. He saw the giant Philistine named Goliath making threats against God's people.

What was David's reaction to Goliath's defiance of God? (See 1 Sam. 17:26,36,45.) *He was offended that he would defy / challenge God's people.*

What surprises you about David's reaction? *He seemed so calm and assured he would win.*

Setting aside everything you already know about David, do you think this reaction to the enemy of God's people meant David would be a good leader? Why or why not? *yes, because he is looking at whats best for God's ppl.*

How did God prepare David for this assignment? How does knowing this part of David's story help you trust that, in your own hard circumstances, God could use this as preparation for a future assignment? *in his shephard skills, he fought bears + lions. This is similar.*

David defeated Goliath, and, from that day on, Saul kept David among his servants, not allowing him to return home. David marched with the troops and became popular among the people, so much so that Saul became jealous of David and attempted to have him killed. For the rest of 1 Samuel, David's greatest enemy was Saul himself. Saul hunted David, the chosen king, for the rest of his life.

I don't want to assign David thoughts and feelings that aren't made clear from the text. However, I can tell you that if I were David and had been anointed the future king, I would have made some assumptions of what God would do with me at that point and how my life would look. I would have assumptions about:

GOD'S TIMING—**I will take the throne quickly.** But as we see from the text, it was years (some commentaries say as many as ten to fifteen years) before David became the ruling king over all of Israel.

GOD'S PROTECTION—**I will be protected from any possible attack from Saul.** As we continue to read the story, we see Saul wanted to kill David and sought to do just that for many years. David could be found hiding in caves and constantly running in fear of his life.

GOD'S PROVISION—**God will surely provide for me solid people to surround me and set me up to succeed in my calling.** In 1 Samuel 22:2 we read a description of the men who surrounded David: "And everyone who was in distress, and everyone who was in debt, and everyone who was bitter in soul, gathered to him. And he became commander over them. And there were with him about 400 men."

If you were David, how would you have struggled at this point in your life? *That's so tough !!*

This is where my trust in God can start to feel shaky—when I make assumptions about God's timing, protection, and provision that don't play out in my life like I thought they would. Because of different seasons I've walked through, I've spent hours in counseling learning how to repair my broken trust with people.

I'll be honest, there are some days when repairing trust feels like an impossible task. Just when I think I'm making progress something triggers a traumatizing memory and the wounds feel fresh all over again. It's been a very "two steps forward, ten steps back, eight steps forward, one step back, two steps forward" kind of progress. If you do the math from that last sentence, progress is being made, but it's slow. And shaky at times.

Trust is hard won for me. But it's doubly hard to rebuild.

I've learned trust is the oxygen of human relationships, and without it, authentic connection can't occur.

An added complication for me is that when my trust was broken in these human relationships, I found a deeper resistance in my heart to trust God as well. I hadn't expected this, but I very much experienced it. It was so hard for me to process how God saw what was happening with these situations and didn't stop any of it.

Gracious, I wish I were sitting down expressing this struggle of mine with you, just the two of us over coffee rather than in these typed words. You'd see tears in my eyes. And maybe I'd see tears in yours as well. Because even if you haven't experienced the same types of hurt that I have, I would imagine you've also experienced God allowing something that's hard for you to process. Some place where you trusted God but then His timing, His protection, or His provision didn't look at all like you thought it would.

You know God is trustworthy, but it doesn't feel like you can personally trust Him with this situation. And that causes a skepticism you don't want to be there in your relationship with Him.

I don't have quick and easy answers for you. But I can tell you I'm learning a lot about what to pursue and what not to pursue in hard life circumstances.

Pursuing answers to why God allows hard things has never given me the peace I want. Honestly, even if God did tell me why, I probably wouldn't see enough of His big picture to agree with Him. I don't think answers to our "why" questions would make our circumstances better or give us a peace in the midst of them.

So, I have to pursue something different. I'm choosing to pursue learning how to daily rely on God in the midst of circumstances that make me resistant to trust.

C. S. Lewis said, "Relying on God has to begin all over again every day as if nothing had yet been done."[3]

> PURSUING ANSWERS TO WHY GOD ALLOWS HARD THINGS HAS NEVER GIVEN ME THE PEACE I WANT.

When we rely on God daily, we can experience the fruit of trust. Scripture outlines a variety of outcomes that will come about as we make the decision to declare our God is trustworthy rather than determine whether or not He's trustworthy because of our circumstances.

Here are some attributes of God we can bank on in declaring He is trustworthy:

- UNCHANGEABLENESS (immutability)—God is unchanging in His being, perfections, purposes, and promises, yet God is not robotic. God does have feelings. He feels love, compassion, righteous anger, and grief. But, unlike humans, His emotions are always in line with His true, sinless character. His character does not shift with His emotions.

- WISDOM (divine intelligence)[4]—God always chooses the best goals and the best means to accomplish those goals.

- KNOWLEDGE (omniscience)—God knows all things in their entirety. There is nothing hidden from God. Because God knows all things and sees all things, only He sees the big picture of which we see in part.

- RIGHTEOUSNESS (justice)—God always acts in accordance with what is right and is Himself the final standard of what is right.

- PEACE (order)—God is not the author of confusion and disorder, yet He is active in the midst of confusion to bring about His eventual fully controlled order.[5]

> Which one of these attributes speaks most deeply to your heart right now?

FRUIT OF TRUSTING GOD

On the next page are some wonderful verses we can incorporate into our prayers, thoughts, and conversations as we pursue relying on God. These speak to the fruit we will experience as we rely on God and stand on the assurance of our trustworthy God. We have to fight the urge to expect our version of God's good timing, God's good provision, and God's good protection to match what we script out for our lives. A big part of learning to rely on a trustworthy God is resetting how we define *good*. Some other words we may have to redefine are *peace* and *security* and *strength* and allow God's definition to invade our reality.

FRUIT	SCRIPTURE
PEACE	Isaiah 26:3-4 (See also Rom. 15:13.)
SECURITY	Psalm 37:3 (See also Ps. 32:10; 125:1; Isa. 28:16; 57:13.)
PROTECTION FROM DANGER	Psalm 31:14-15; 32:7; 33:18-22; 91:1-4
FREEDOM FROM FEAR	Psalm 125:1; Proverbs 29:25
PROVISION	Proverbs 28:25 (See also Jer. 17:7-8.)
STRENGTH	Isaiah 30:15; 40:29-31

Now back to David's story. What I would have assumed David's reality to be and what it actually looked like several years after being anointed king are vastly different.

Read 1 Samuel 24:3-15. What opportunity did David have in the cave? What did David's actions say about his character and trust in God?

He could have killed Saul but instead cut his robe proving he could have died. He trusted God would take care of the situation.

Have you ever had the opportunity to get revenge—however small? How did you handle the situation?

Looking back on the situation you thought of in the previous question, how does this relate to a bigger decision to trust God or not?

The Book of 1 Samuel ends with Saul and his sons dead on the battlefield.

Read 2 Samuel 5:1-5. How long did David reign in Judah? *7yr 6 months* And in Jerusalem? *33 yrs*

David became king of Israel and shortly after moved his headquarters to Jerusalem. He united the northern tribes with the southern tribes under one crown. He moved the ark of the covenant to Jerusalem too. David desired to build God a temple to dwell in.

Read 2 Samuel 7:1-17. What did David ask to do for God? *Build a house for the ark of covenant*

What did God promise to do for David? *Be w/him + his kingdom will endure forever*

Who would build a house for God? *David*

What was the promise God made in verse 16? How is this pointing to Jesus? (Look at Luke 1:31-33.) *your kindom will endure forever.*

Scripture refers to David as "a man after [God's] own heart" (1 Sam. 13:14; Acts 13:22). Knowing this—and knowing that David wrote many beautiful psalms in the Bible and that from his lineage King Jesus was born—can make us feel like David was superhuman, almost too perfect, and hard to relate to. However, David was not a perfect man. If you know much about the rest of his story, there was a season of his life that looked more like a reality TV show gone bad than something you would see in the Bible.

David got distracted, was tempted, and then entered into a situation you'd never picture him in. He committed adultery and then orchestrated a murder to cover it up. But can I whisper something from the depths of my heart? Being able to see David's eventual humble response to his sins in Psalm 51 helps me. His frailties give me a safe place to admit and process my own. His sin helps shed light on my own. And His redemption helps give me hope for my own.

Ultimately, being able to see God's response to David, still calling him a man after His own heart despite his failings, deepens my trust in God. There were still really hard consequences unleashed by his sin, but God's grace paved the way to an amazing legacy.

Read Psalm 51. List a few lines from the psalm that speak to your heart today.

How does David's story of sin and repentance give you hope for your story? *Create in me a pure heart, O God. & renew a steadfast spirit within me.*

We see so much emotion wrapped up in the words of Psalm 51 as well as many of the other psalms David wrote. Emotions are powerful.

In hard situations, do you typically process emotionally and then spiritually? Or spiritually and then emotionally? Write some thoughts about this below. *emotionally then spiritually*

What is a strong emotion you feel that could show you are not trusting God? *nervous / unease of the future doubt*

And on the flip side of that, what is a strong emotion you feel that shows you *are* trusting God?
peace, calmness,

It's important here to recognize that our human emotion is not discounted by truth. For example, just because we know the truth does not mean we do not doubt. Rather, we can fully experience doubt, but we filter it through the truth, which should allow us to respond to our doubt in faith. We can fully feel the feeling, but the expression of what we feel needs to be fueled by faith, which produces hope in our trustworthy King.

David knew what sin was like, and he knew forgiveness. Before David's death, he passed on both God's promises and His instructions to his son Solomon.

Read 1 Kings 2:1-12. What were David's last instructions to his son Solomon?

Follow God's laws to keep God's promise to him that his descendents would always have a seat on the throne
+ punish enemies to establish his reign.

What is the promise David referred to in verse 4?

What do you think this promise means?

God will protect + be w/ his family + people always

Flip to the New Testament and read Matthew 1:1. Whose Son is Jesus?

David

Jesus is the Son of David. He is the King of kings. He will be the One God sends to save His people.

King SOLOMON

One of the most exciting moments of my life was the birth of my firstborn daughter. Part of the reason was the sheer nature of welcoming a new life into the world. But another reason for the excitement for us that day was that we had been told we were having a boy!

So our planned name of Andrew Cole had to be quickly reconsidered.

We landed on the name Hope, which for us was layered with meaning both biblical and personal. I loved Jeremiah 29:11, and, though I didn't understand the full meaning of the verse, I loved the words dancing around the theme of hope. But also, personally, Hope was born in the midst of a hard time in our marriage. Seeing God bring life into our world through this delightful child made the name Hope all the more fitting.

Names are important. And the naming of David and Bathsheba's son was no exception. Solomon, later to become King Solomon, was the wisest king to ever live. However, before Solomon was ever known for his wisdom, and before he was even king, his story started in the midst of pain.

   Read 2 Samuel 12:13-25.

Solomon was not King David and Bathsheba's first child. Their first child died as a result of their sin. I want to pause here and say I know that statement hits hard for some of us. It does for me too. Next week in the Digging Deeper section we look at the death of another son because of his father's sin. I'd encourage you to flip ahead and read that segment if you need to today. Especially if you have lost a child or a loved one, these two stories can seem confusing and maybe even disillusioning. Why would a loving God do something so harsh and seemingly unfair? I can't provide full answers, but I hope by exploring these tragedies together we can learn even more about God's character and His goodness no matter what.

In David and Bathsheba's case, God graciously provided another son, Solomon.

When you look in your Bible, your footnote may say that Solomon's name means "peace" (v. 24). This helps us to see that God intended for there to be peace. As we look deeper into the Hebrew, based on some recent studies we find that Solomon's name is derived from the Hebrew word שלם *(shillem)* which means "to replace or restore."[6]

> Keeping that meaning in mind, why do you think David and Bathsheba named their son Solomon?
>
> *Because he brought peace to their heartache + replaced their 1st son.*

Solomon was the gracious gift God gave to bring restoration to David and Bathsheba in the midst of their pain.

> In verse 25, what other name was given to Solomon? What does this other name mean? (Look in the footnotes of your Bible for help.)
>
> *Jedidiah – means loved by God.*

> Why do you think Solomon was also given that name?
>
> *because he was loved*

Here's what we don't know: Depending on the translation you read, it can appear like God gave Solomon the name Jedidiah. That's the way it appears when I read these verses in the NIV. But the ESV has different punctuation, which could lead us to believe it could be David saying the boy should be called Jedidiah.

So, here's what we do know about Solomon's name: He is called Solomon. Based on all that we've studied about the naming of Solomon (Jedidiah) we can know from the beginning of his life he was both a gift of restoration for David and Bathsheba, used by God to establish peace within Israel during his reign, and he was deeply loved by God.

But make no mistake, though there was restoration, there was not long-term peace in this family. In 2 Samuel 12:10, the Lord spoke to David through the prophet Nathan, "Now therefore the sword shall never depart from your house, because you have despised me and have taken the wife of Uriah the Hittite [Bathsheba] to be your wife."

Solomon was only one of King David's nineteen sons (1 Chron. 3:1-9). Needless to say, competition for David's throne was fierce. The competition starts before King David's death (1 Kings 1) and finishes with Solomon being named king and ascending to the throne (1 Kings 2:12).

Look at 1 Kings 1–2:17 and answer the following questions.

Why did Adonijah think he should be king? (See 1 Kings 2:15.)

Because he was older & claimed it 1st

From your study so far and your knowledge of the rest of Scripture, name some other times God chose someone other than the obvious for a position.

David & Goliath
Ruth
Jesus

What did Adonijah attempt to do in order to become king?

Gather all the people
make sacrifices

How did Adonijah react when he was told Solomon had been made king of Israel?

He didn't want to die

Solomon agreed to spare Adonijah's life but on the condition that he "show himself a worthy man" (1 Kings 1:52). Sadly, Adonijah showed himself to be wicked and deceptive. Adonijah, through Bathsheba, asked for the hand of Abishag, the Shunammite woman who served King David on his deathbed. On the surface, this seemed like no big deal. Maybe Adonijah was ready to settle down and start a family, and he really liked Abishag. However, there was subtle deception in this request.

Adonijah asked for a woman who was in the court of King Solomon, and if he took her as his wife this could be seen as an act of attempting to claim the kingship from Solomon! Remember Solomon's condition for Adonijah's safety? Adonijah showed his wickedness, and, as a result, he was sentenced to death.

With Adonijah's death, Solomon sat securely as the third king of Israel.

Read 1 Kings 3:3-14. In your own words, how would you define *wisdom?* *discernment to do whats right*

WE ALL NEED WISDOM STRAIGHT FROM GOD—FOR DECISION-MAKING, FOR HELPING OTHERS, FOR UNDERSTANDING ANOTHER PERSON'S VIEWPOINT.

Why do you think Solomon asked for wisdom? And how does his request highlight his trust in God at that point in his life?

Because there's big decisions as king

Why was it good for him to request wisdom?

He needed it

We'll read more about Solomon in the days to come, but I've always been struck by his request. Even though he was a newly crowned king, he didn't ask for strength or admiration or even negotiating skills. He asked for wisdom. We all need wisdom straight from God—for decision-making, for helping others, for understanding another person's viewpoint.

Shechem

Before you close your Bible study today, spend a moment asking God for wisdom. Maybe you need wisdom for a specific situation or maybe you want to ask for wisdom to guard your heart and mind every day. Think about how using God's wisdom instead of your own opinions is a good demonstration of trusting God. And lastly, thank Him for giving you understanding and truth.

the

TEMPLE

I am a planner. A problem-solver. So when I bring my struggles to the Lord in prayer, I tend to also bring my carefully thought-out ideas and suggestions He can choose from.

Here's what I think will work, Lord. I just need You to sign off on one of these, okay?

But the longer I walk with Him, the more I discover that isn't the way God works. His ways? They aren't our ways. And that's actually something we should be thankful for, even when He asks us to do things that don't make sense to us.

In looking at the life of Solomon, we see he started out trusting God and honoring His ways. Early on in his reign, we find him lifting up a completely God-honoring prayer full of trust during one of the most pivotal times in his kingdom—the dedication of the temple.

Solomon's monumental achievement was the construction of the temple of God. For all of King David's tremendous achievements and accomplishments, the one thing he was not able to accomplish was the construction of the temple. God didn't allow David to build the temple because David was a man of war and bloodshed (1 Chron. 22:8; 28:3). This can appear like an unfair consequence. After all, most of the battles David fought were in obedience to God. But consider this: the task of building the temple wasn't an assignment God gave to David and then took away from him after all the battles. Building the temple was David's request (2 Sam. 7:2), a request God denied.

David's desire to build the temple was a good thing, which can make it feel like a good idea. But not all good ideas are God ideas. When we find ourselves in similar situations, we have yet another opportunity to make the choice to trust God.

> Read 1 Kings 8:17-18. Wanting to build the temple was a right desire in David's heart but it wasn't the right timing with God. How does this apply to something in your life right now?
>
> *My business / organized home*
>
> *Having Eli*

God gave the task, responsibility, and privilege of building the temple to Solomon.

The actual construction of the temple can be found in 1 Kings 6:1–9:10.

> As you look at 1 Kings 6:1–9:10, does anything from the construction of the temple surprise you or stand out?
>
> *So much details - gold + bronze + decorations. Cedar lining the whole inside - no stone showing.*

> Look at the temple infographic on the next page. What are some things that stand out to you about the temple itself? (If you have extra time this week, feel free to do further research on the areas of the temple that stood out to you.) *women on outside*

When the construction was complete, King Solomon dedicated the temple (1 Kings 8).

> Read 1 Kings 8:22-53.

The Temple

1. Holy of Holies
2. Holy Place
3. Veil
4. Altar of Incense
5. Table of Showbread
6. Seven-branched Lampstand
7. Court of Priests
8. Court of Israel (men)
9. Altar of Burnt Offerings
10. Animal Preparation Area
11. East Gate
12. Court of Women
13. Women's Balconies

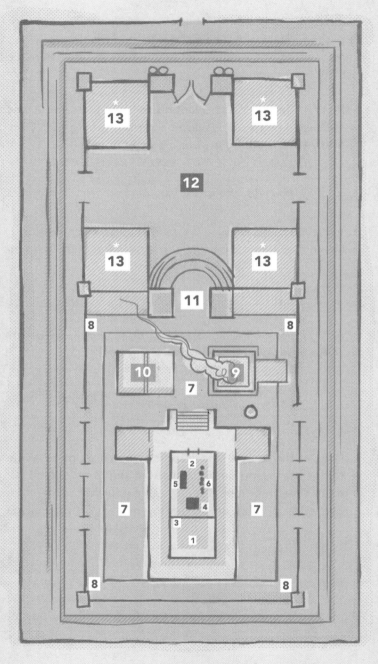

As we read Solomon's prayer, let's pay close attention to both the words of the prayer and its structure. Solomon used three different Hebrew words for prayer, which each have their own meaning. Underline in your Bible or note these words as you read through the verses.

1. Intercession and praise (vv. 28-30,33,35);

2. Plea for mercy or help (vv. 38,45);

3. Cry of joy or sorrow (v. 52).[7]

Clearly, we see the intense emotion of Solomon in his prayer. All of the emotion leads us to the essence of his prayer—two very important realities.

1. Humanity's pattern is waywardness.

2. God's pattern is covenant commitment and steadfast grace.

When have you seen these two realities collide in your life or in the life of someone you know? Write about one of those times.

it's easy to get distracted + loose sight of God as #1. whenI'm struggling, then I turn to God, for sure.

Throughout this prayer, King Solomon seemed to anticipate all the ways the people of God could (and would) sin and wander away from Him (vv. 31-51). Solomon's prayer can be broken down into seven specific petitions, and in each of these instances we see the propensity and pattern of Israel turning away from the Lord. Solomon, however, reminded the people that even in the midst of their unfaithfulness, God would remain faithful to all those who would be repentant and turn toward Him. Solomon described just this when he referred to the "covenant of love" (v. 23, NIV). The Hebrew word translated as "love" is *hesed*, which refers to the loyalty or unbroken nature of God's covenant.[8] Another translation of this Hebrew word is "steadfast"—*hesed* is the steadfast love of God.

How would you define the word *steadfast?* Why is it important that our God's love is steadfast?

Steady - constant nor matter what

The ending of Solomon's prayer (vv. 52-53) is as important as the beginning (v. 23). King Solomon started by declaring the covenant-keeping character of God based on the promise God made to David, and he ended by referencing the covenant promises God made to Moses.

Look up Exodus 19:5 and Deuteronomy 7:6. What did God promise to Moses?

to protect his ppl.

All of Scripture anticipates the coming of Jesus and His kingdom. The beauty of Scripture is seeing how the will and desire of God for reconciliation and unity among the nations is woven throughout. For instance, one of the petitions we find in Solomon's prayer is a petition for the foreigner that "they shall hear of your great name" (1 Kings 8:42a). We see God's greater redemptive plan to save and rescue both Jew and Gentile even here in 1 Kings.

How would the foreigner hear of the great name of the Lord? They would hear it through God's people, who would be a witness to all humanity. Jesus described something very similar in Matthew 5:14-16 when He called the people of God "a city set on a hill." What a glorious privilege and responsibility for us today to make known the great name of our Lord!

What does it practically look like to be a city on a hill? Who inspires you to be this way?

Sharing God w/everyone
Jane

In 1 Kings chapter 9, we see God's response after Solomon completed the temple and dedicated it.

God appeared to Solomon and reminded him of the unconditional promise He made to David (v. 5).

Read 1 Kings 9:6, and then list some of the consequences found in verses 7-9.

If they turn away from God, he will exile them from their land + reject the temple.

In verse 6, there is a significant shift from unconditional to conditional. God reminded Solomon of not only his responsibility but the responsibility of the Israelites to turn to God and remain faithful. The language of this address shifts from second person singular (you) to second person plural (in the southern United States, we'd say y'all) to include all the people within this covenant responsibility. Essentially, as Solomon led, so the Israelites would follow. As Solomon trusted, the Israelites would be prone to trust. As Solomon slipped into distrust, the Israelites would follow into wayward and distrustful living.

After having some amazing encounters with God, why do you think Solomon still slipped into disobedience and distrust?

worldly influence
life got easier

Have you ever been in a situation where you were tempted to place your trust in others or yourself above God? Explain.

yes

I don't know what situation is begging you to put your trust in yourself or your own desires above the Lord. I don't know what steps of obedience God is currently calling you to take. But let me be the gentle whisper in your ear encouraging you to keep going. Keep trusting. Keep taking step after obedient step.

We don't have to understand the why of God's ways. But we do have to keep choosing to follow them.

Let's not stop short of our victory with God. He is working things out. He is present. His plan is still good, and He can still be trusted. These are true certainties even when life feels so very uncertain.

> WE DON'T HAVE TO UNDERSTAND THE WHY OF GOD'S WAYS. BUT WE DO HAVE TO KEEP CHOOSING TO FOLLOW THEM.

the WIVES

I don't think anyone wakes up and says, "I'm going to make a total mess of my life today. I plan to purposefully ignore all the wisdom God has ever given me, sin like crazy, and ruin all that I hold dear."[9]

No, I think the unraveling of a life starts slowly. Much like what happened to one of my favorite sweaters. It was the kind of sweater that snagged easily if I wasn't careful. For the longest time, I was mindful of the delicate nature of this sweater, protecting it so I could make it last and enjoy wearing it time and again.

But one day I got in a hurry and pulled a huge snag in it. And instead of taking the time to properly repair it, I snipped the loose threads and hoped for the best. That decision started an unraveling process that ruined my sweater.

I believe this is where we find King Solomon today—forgetting to carefully guard his heart (Prov. 4:23) and making choices that ultimately led to the unraveling of his faithfulness to God.

As we've seen, Solomon started out well. He was a king who sought the Lord for wisdom. He built the temple and prayerfully dedicated it to the Lord. He was a greatly accomplished man, with a palace brimming with riches and a heart so overflowing with wisdom that people from all over the world sought an audience with him (1 Kings 10:23-24).

But Solomon had an area of sin that became a snagging point for him in his relationship with the Lord.

According to 1 Kings 11:1, what was Solomon's snagging point?

women from other nations that God warned would lead you astray.

This was a big issue because God commanded His people not to intermarry.

Read Deuteronomy 7:3-6. Why did God command His people not to intermarry with those outside of the nation of Israel?

they worshipped other Gods + would lead you astray.

Not only did God command His people not to intermarry, but He had spoken this directly to Solomon twice, both at Gibeon and after the temple was finished.

You cannot enter into an intimate love relationship with someone without that person not only affecting your mind and your body but also your soul.

Sadly, despite all the wisdom Solomon had been given, he still gave in to the sinful desires of his heart. This king, who prayed during the temple dedication that the Lord would turn the hearts of the people of Israel toward Himself (1 Kings 8:58), clung to his forbidden wives and ended up with his own heart being turned away from the Lord (1 Kings 11:2-3).

It would be easy for us to focus on the dysfunctional family dynamics that Solomon had to deal with. However, as we consider the events that took place during Solomon's ascension to the throne, we could miss a subtle character trait of Solomon that we will see in greater clarity throughout his life. Solomon's reaction to Adonijah's request to take Abishag as his wife was drastic and filled with emotion, anger, and violence. And as we look deeper, we will find that Solomon had a soft spot for women.

For all the riches, power, and might God had provided Solomon, the king still experienced deep distrust in God. Solomon's decision to cling to his wives is evidence of his distrust that God could be the source of his satisfaction. If Solomon's response to Adonijah's request for Abishag tunes our ears to the possibility of a character flaw, Solomon's marriage to Pharaoh's daughter (1 Kings 3:1) is the first chord struck that enables us to hear the sound of sorrow that would follow.

could be me. what are you clinging to?

Solomon's many marriages to foreign women went directly against God's direction, warning the people of Israel that their hearts would be turned away from the Lord their God as a result of these marriages (1 Kings 11:2). Again, evidence of distrust in God's goodness. It's important to note that the issue wasn't an ethnicity issue in marriage; it was an issue of idolatry and turning hearts toward false gods.

Read 1 Kings 11:4. What happened to Solomon?

His ♡ was swayed

I find it so interesting that this Scripture verse references Solomon's father, David. As we noted previously, David was also a man whose heart had been led astray by his sinful desire for a woman. His "snagging" point was not so different from his son's, leading David to commit sin upon sin upon sin (2 Sam. 11). But instead of being labeled a man who did evil in the sight of the Lord as Solomon was (1 Kings 11:6), David was called a man after God's own heart (1 Sam. 13:14).

Why do you think David was still called a man after God's own heart while Solomon was labeled differently?

David repented

David's response to his sin was quite different from Solomon's response. Read 2 Samuel 12:1-14 and compare it to what we have already read in Psalm 51 (Day 2). What do these sections of Scripture tell us about David's response to his sin?

he repented

David owned his sin. He chose to repair the breach in his relationship with God using the thread of repentance—confessing his sins and placing his affection and his devotion firmly on the Lord once again.

Solomon continued in his sin. His refusal to repent and realign his desires with the Lord's resulted in God's declaration that He would tear the kingdom away from Solomon during the rule of his son. Solomon's legacy would not be all God had originally designed and desired it to be (1 Kings 11:9-12).

Oh, sweet friends, God's reminders to us in today's passages should not be taken lightly. God isn't after our earthly accomplishments. And He doesn't want us going through the motions of devotion. He's after our hearts. God wants to be our soul's sole desire. And the minute we turn our hearts away from God is the minute our intimacy with Him and our legacy begins to unravel.

This is exactly what takes place with Solomon, especially in his old age. Solomon's love, affection, and trust shifted from God to his wives and their gods.

One of the saddest sentences in 1 Kings may be the most overlooked sentence. First Kings 11:4b says, "And his heart was not wholly true to the LORD his God, as was the heart of David his father." In this one sentence we see that Solomon is one of many kings on a journey of half-hearted trust. Really, half-hearted trust is simply distrust.

Before we end today's study, let's do a recap of the time line of Solomon's affections.

HALF-HEARTED TRUST IS SIMPLY DISTRUST.

- He worshiped at the high places as was acceptable because the temple of God did not yet exist (1 Kings 3:2).

- He gained wisdom from God (1 Kings 3:5-14).

- He left the high places to worship God at the ark of the covenant (1 Kings 3:15).

- He built the temple and placed the ark inside of it (1 Kings 5–8).

- He turned away from godly wisdom (1 Kings 11:1-4).

- He returned to the high places, now condemned, and defied God (1 Kings 11:5-8).[10]

After the temple was built, all of the high places should have been destroyed! But they weren't.

Important note: High places, prior to the construction of the temple, were acceptable places of worship as long as they were used to glorify God. A high place means a place of worship. It looked like a stage or a platform where religious activities took place. The danger with the Israelites' use of the high places was that they lived with an awareness of how other cultures worshiped false gods. These other nations also built high places, but they were for worshiping false gods and often included practices that were highly detestable in God's sight.

So, after the temple was built, that should have been the designated place of worship for the Israelites. The other high places should have been torn down as God repeatedly instructed His people to do.

This begs the question, why didn't Solomon destroy these high places? By allowing the high places to stay standing, the people were tempted to use them as alternate places to worship, which was dishonoring to God. But even more disturbing, we also see the Israelites following some of the practices of surrounding pagan nations to try and get specific needs met apart from trusting God. For example, going to a high place for the fertility god if they were struggling to get pregnant or worshiping Baal, the thunder god, when they were concerned about a lack of rain.

WHEN WE LET THE HIGH PLACES STAND, WE ARE INVITING TEMPTATION TO CAPTIVATE OUR HEARTS.

Think about this in the context of our lives. Are there places we turn when we don't think God is coming through for us and we're struggling to trust Him?

This is true for our own stories. God is asking us to destroy all the high places in our lives. When we let these places stand, we are inviting temptation to captivate our hearts.

Take a moment to pray, asking the Lord to reveal anything that holds your affection more than Him. Take the time to repair those seemingly small snags—the ones that can have devastating consequences—by going to God in repentance. Humility beautifully ties the knot between our hearts and His.

MAP OF
the
HIGH PLACES

○ TEL DAN

Sea of Galilee

MT. CARMEL ∧

∧ MT. TABOR

Mediterranean Sea

ISRAEL

∧ GERIZIM

◎ SHILOH

◎ OPHRAH   ◎ BOCHIM

◎ BETHEL
◎ MIZPAH

◎ GIBEON

JERUSALEM ◎   ◎ GIBEAH   GILGAL ◎
UNNAMED HILL ◎   ◎ NOB
                          ◎ KIRJATH-JEARIM
BETHLEHEM ◎

The Dead Sea

HEBRON ◎

1. List of High Places adapted from *The New Schaff-Herzog Encyclopedia of Religious Knowledge: Embracing Biblical, Historical, Doctrinal, and Practical Theology and Biblical, Theological, and Ecclesiastical Biography from the Earliest Times to the Present Day* (New York; London: Funk & Wagnalls, 1908–1914), 277.

WORD STUDY:
TRUSTWORTHY

One of the most constant themes we see throughout Scripture is the truth that God is trustworthy. The actual English word *trustworthy* only shows up a handful of times in the Bible; however, the truth of God's trustworthy character is evident in every page of Scripture.[11] Throughout the story of Scripture, we see evidence of this truth in God's covenant promises made to Abraham, Moses, and David.

Take a moment and recollect images of God's faithfulness. When we remember His faithfulness, we come to believe that because God is faithful, He can be trusted. In other words, He is trustworthy. God promised Abraham that his children would be like the stars in the sky and the sand on the seashore. This comes true and is one of the reasons why the Egyptians feared the Israelites and eventually turned them into slaves. God promised Abraham the land of Canaan, and through Moses the Israelites were led out of captivity toward the land God had promised.

Think about every instance and evidence of God's trustworthy nature in the wilderness wandering. God went before them in a pillar of fire by night and cloud by day. God rested in the midst of their presence in the tabernacle. God provided them manna to eat. Every need of the Israelites was met. Yet, there was one thing God did that outshines every other example. One very specific deed done that exemplifies His trustworthy nature. God was faithful to the promise He made to Adam and Eve by crushing the head of the serpent as He sent His own Son to earth to die the death we should have died. Jesus reigns victorious over sin and death.

This is why the psalmist could truthfully declare in Psalm 111:7,

> The works of his hands are faithful and just;
>
> all his precepts are trustworthy.

The Hebrew word for *trustworthy* comes from the root word אמן (*'á·mân*) and encapsulates loyalty, faithfulness, and dependability—all characteristics that are true and evident in God. In one sentence the psalmist declared that all of God's works are faithful and filled with justice; therefore, He is trustworthy. When we read about trust in the Old Testament, we will also come across the Hebrew word **bāṭaḥ**, which is a parallel to **āman**.[12] When we trust *(bāṭaḥ/āman)* in someone or something, we are typically looking for a source of security to rely on. In the Old Testament it's interesting to see that whenever the object of our trust is God, we are commanded to trust (Ps. 4:5; 37:3; 62:8; 115:9; Prov. 3:5; Isa. 26:4). However, when the object of trust is humanity or human-made objects, these terms have negative implications (Ps. 41:9; 146:3; Jer. 9:4; 46:25).

When we come to the New Testament, the root word for trust is πιστός *(pistós)* and refers to being worthy of belief, faithful, and dependable. It can even elicit the response of trust or faith. Of the roughly sixty-seven occurrences of πιστός *(pistós)*, forty-five instances translate to "faith" or "faithful."[13] Nine instances translate literally as "trustworthy" (1 Cor. 7:25; 1 Tim. 1:15; 3:1; 4:9; 2 Tim. 2:11; Titus 1:9; 3:8; Rev. 21:5; Rev. 22:6).[14]

I don't think it's a coincidence that the apostle Paul commended his disciples to be reminded of the trustworthy nature of the gospel and Jesus. To Timothy, he said, "The saying is trustworthy and deserving of full acceptance" (1 Tim. 4:9). To Titus he pled, "He must hold firm to the trustworthy word as taught" (Titus 1:9). These encouragements are so applicable to us today. We need this very reminder. We need to be reminded of Revelation 22:6, "And he said to me, 'these words are trustworthy and true.'" In order to experience the hope of these trustworthy words, we must know the Word. As we rehearse the truth of the faithful character and nature of God, we will be filled with hope, which will elicit active and obedient faith in our trustworthy God.

WATCH VIDEO SESSION 2 AND RECORD YOUR NOTES BELOW.

Solomon-

Was humble when he was crowned King-
I don't know how to do _____ even thought have
all the qualification. Ask God to help you.

We will become like what we focus on - what we
re-vere - reflect on

He idolized the idols more than God.

High places were regular part of routine.

Sometimes our high places are our delisions that
we can fix/do/handle the issues all on our own.
on

the temple took 7 yrs.
His personal palace took 13 yrs. - He was making space for
all his wives that he was told not to have anyway"

I King ll Now, Pharo
Do I trust God enough to bring my distrust/overwhelm/
etc? or do I turn to other things to soothe/fix/forget?

VIDEO GROUP DISCUSSION QUESTIONS

After watching the video, discuss the following questions in your group.

- What are some of the ways that Solomon started out as a strong leader?

- What was Solomon's mistake in 1 Kings 3:3 that hindered his leadership and his life?

- We may not worship idols or at the high places in the same way Solomon did, but what are our modern-day idols? What are the things that pull us away from God?

- What are some of the consequences of misplaced affections?

- What do you learn from Solomon that challenges you to live differently?

- How can you replace maintaining personal control with trusting God in your own life? What are ways you can lean upon God more than yourself?

 **To access the video teaching sessions,** use the instructions in the back of your Bible study book.

51

Rehoboam
AND Jeroboam

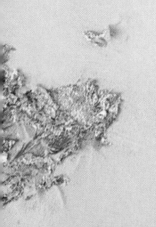

WEEK 2

I TRUST IN THE STEADFAST LOVE OF GOD FOREVER AND EVER.

PSALM 52:8b

#TRUSTWORTHYSTUDY

Connecting the Kings

Toward the end of King Solomon's life, we find that his heart was divided between affections for his wives and God. Ultimately, King Solomon's divided heart resulted in a divided kingdom. This didn't happen until his son Rehoboam was seated on the throne. Rehoboam saw in his father a desire for personal gain rather than a compassionate care for the people, and the people rebelled. Now, we're going to go into these stories in further detail in your homework this week, but for the sake of connecting the kings, here's a quick overview.

The Israelite people and Jeroboam, a former administrator for King Solomon, pleaded with King Rehoboam to soften the heavy burden placed on them by Solomon. Rehoboam asked for three days to consider the request. Rehoboam wisely inquired of the older men (1 Kings 12:6-8). The elders tried to teach and train Rehoboam to be a godly king and to serve God's people. Rehoboam's response was to abandon this advice and take up the advice of the young men, who suggested the burden increase (1 Kings 12:10-11). This fateful decision led to the eventual division of the kingdom. Just as the prophet Ahijah prophesied (1 Kings 11:29-32), the kingdom was torn in two. The ten northern tribes of Israel rejected Rehoboam as king and established Jeroboam as king. The two southern tribes stayed loyal to Rehoboam and formed the Southern Kingdom. What was once a united kingdom was now divided. How tragic![15]

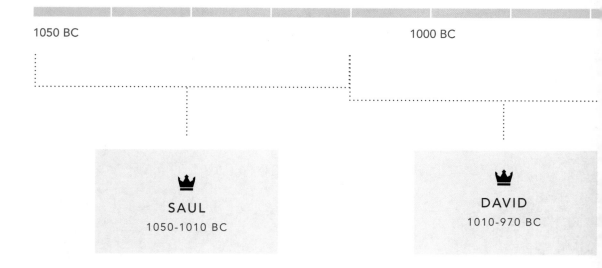

1050 BC

1000 BC

♔ SAUL
1050-1010 BC

♔ DAVID
1010-970 BC

To study more about the kings, please see the Guide to 1 & 2 Kings on page 207.

*Please note: The dates listed below are the approximate years each king reigned. Due to co-regency and other variables, these dates may vary by source.

NORTHERN KINGDOM TRIBES

ASHER	MANASSEH
DAN	NAPHTALI
EPHRAIM	REUBEN
GAD	ZEBULUN
SIMEON	
ISSACHAR	

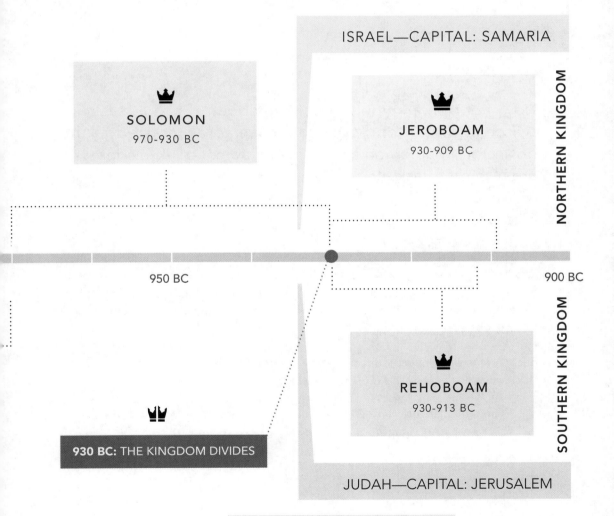

ISRAEL—CAPITAL: SAMARIA

NORTHERN KINGDOM

👑
SOLOMON
970-930 BC

👑
JEROBOAM
930-909 BC

950 BC

900 BC

SOUTHERN KINGDOM

👑
REHOBOAM
930-913 BC

👑
930 BC: THE KINGDOM DIVIDES

JUDAH—CAPITAL: JERUSALEM

SOUTHERN KINGDOM TRIBES

JUDAH
BENJAMIN

Faithlife Study Bible (Bellingham, WA: Lexham Press, 2012), 2016.

JEROBOAM'S
Great POTENTIAL

Now, I don't want you to think I'm about to pull a bait-and-switch situation on you, but I have to acknowledge the downside of Solomon asking for wisdom. I think wisdom is a great thing to ask for—we even wrote out a prayer for more wisdom in our lives. But what I see in Solomon's life, the wisest man alive during his time, was that wisdom could only take him so far.

Wisdom gave him incredible leadership insights. Wisdom gave him brilliance admired by people near and far. Wisdom gave him keen discernment for settling issues between people in a dispute. Wisdom gave him knowledge he could use to carry out every duty required of him.

But it seems wisdom without obedience to God does not produce the kind of life God wants us to lead. The Bible makes this clear.

> "'Cursed be anyone who does not confirm the words of this law *by doing them*.' And all the people shall say, 'Amen.'"
>
> DEUTERONOMY 27:26 (EMPHASIS MINE)

And Samuel said,

"Has the LORD as great delight in burnt offerings and sacrifices,

    as in obeying the voice of the LORD?

Behold, to obey is better than sacrifice,

    and to listen than the fat of rams.

For rebellion is as the sin of divination,

    and presumption is as iniquity and idolatry.

Because you have rejected the word of the LORD,

    he has also rejected you from being king."

1 SAMUEL 15:22-23

Read Philippians 4:9 and record what is given to those who put into practice the Word of the Lord.

God will be w/ you.

Also read Luke 6:49 and record what happens when we don't put the Word of the Lord into practice. *we will crumble w/ adversity.*

It's not enough to receive wisdom, have wisdom, teach wisdom, or preach wisdom. We must do what the Word of the Lord says personally and authentically. As I have continued to study the lives of these kings, I am struck by how even small deviations from obedience to God lead to devastations in the long run. Yes, there is mercy. Yes, there is grace. But I much prefer to walk in obedience and have the peace of God than anything that any deviation from the Word of God could ever give me.

I often find myself praying for peace. Wanting peace. Working for peace in my relationships. But sometimes, out of fear or selfish desires, I pursue solutions of my own making more than waiting on God's way or God's timing. I don't want to call it disobedience, nor do I want to attribute it to distrust, but that's exactly what it is for me. I'm not trying to put anything on you, but maybe just consider if any of this resonates with you in some situation you are currently in.

I'm in a season of healing right now where forgiveness is something I know I need to work on in order to be obedient to God's Word. And while I've made huge strides toward forgiving those who have asked for forgiveness, I'm finding myself resistant to forgive those who not only haven't apologized but others who haven't even acknowledged they hurt me. It's all a process, but I can honestly confess that my being resistant with some people is hindering my peace.

If I refuse to cooperate in obedience, I am refusing to be a recipient of God's peace.

That's what I see in Solomon, Rehoboam, and Jeroboam this week. They sacrificed their peace on the altar of their disobedience.

You read in Connecting the Kings that Solomon had a desire for personal gain rather than compassionate care for the people toward the end of his life. We see this played out in the people of Israel being taxed heavily and forced to physically labor to build both the temple and Solomon's palace.

> Read 1 Samuel 8:10-22 and remember what God warned the people that the king would take from them. *He said they would be put to work + taxed + burdened.*
> Read 1 Kings 5:13. Where did Solomon get his laborers?
>
> *All Isreal*
> *30,000 men!*

Now, don't get confused by what you might read later on in 1 Kings 9:21-22. The foreigners were made slaves. The Israelites weren't slaves but were forced laborers who suffered from years of harsh work.

> To set the stage for today's lesson, read 1 Kings 11:26-43.

In 1 Kings 11:26, we meet a man named Jeroboam. King Solomon saw potential, skill, and ability in Jeroboam and appointed him as commissioner for the house of Joseph. Jeroboam essentially served in the royal administration of King Solomon's household. While serving King Solomon, Jeroboam saw how Solomon placed a heavy yoke on his people. Solomon's behavior was self-serving and the people suffered. After watching this oppression, Jeroboam attempted to help the people.[16]

What did Jeroboam do in verse 27?

He built terraces + filled in the gap in the wall of City of David.

"Lifting up his hand" means he stood up to the leadership by attempting a revolt.

Look again at 1 Kings 11:29-39.

When Ahijah tore his robe into twelve pieces, he told Jeroboam to take ten pieces. This was symbolic of how the ten tribes would lead from the torn, divided kingdom that was yet to be formed. Jeroboam would be king over those tribes (v. 31). Now, I bet you're asking what happened to the other pieces. Aren't they representative of the other two tribes in the Southern Kingdom? The other two pieces do represent the Southern Kingdom of Judah. First Kings 11:32 says, "But he [Solomon] shall have one tribe, for the sake of my servant David and for the sake of Jerusalem, the city that I have chosen out of all the tribes of Israel." (Note of clarification: These two pieces represented the tribes of Judah ["for the sake of my servant David] and Benjamin—which included the city of Jerusalem ["for the sake of Jerusalem"].)

GOD IS FAITHFUL TO KEEP HIS PROMISES DESPITE THE UNFAITHFULNESS OF HIS PEOPLE.

Turn to 2 Samuel 7:16. What did God promise David?

Your house + kingdom will endure forever

How does this promise shed light on 1 Kings 11:32?

David Keeps a tiny bit because of God's promise

After Solomon died, David's grandson, Rehoboam, reigned over the tribes of Judah and Benjamin, which was evidence of the faithfulness of God in keeping His promise (despite the unfaithfulness of His people).

Now turn to 1 Samuel 15:24-29. What did Samuel prophesy to Saul? What symbol is used?

Cloak to tear the kingdom

What do these echoes from previous stories in Scripture teach us about God and how we can trust what He says?

He does what he says he does & doesn't △ his mind

These rich connections once again show us of the intentionality of God in reminding His people of His ultimate, sovereign control.

Look at 1 Kings 11:40. What does this tell us about the state of Solomon's heart? *He tried to kill Jeroboam.*

Solomon sought to kill Jeroboam, which is yet more shocking evidence of the spiritual decline of Solomon's heart. He thought he could thwart God's will (as prophesied by Ahijah) and prevent Jeroboam from becoming king, but he was unsuccessful. Once again, God's sovereign will overrode human desire. Another reason God is so very trustworthy—He cannot be manipulated by human actions.

How is this comforting to you in light of the complexities of today's culture and political climate? *God will reign*

As a result of Solomon's wrath, Jeroboam fled and found asylum in Egypt.

That's where we'll end today. But the story is far from over! Tomorrow, we'll learn more about Rehoboam, Jeroboam, and—*cue the dark, foreshadowing music*—how the kingdom divides.

REHOBOAM'S *folly*
Jeroboam's RISE

After Solomon's death, Jeroboam was summoned by the people to deliver the Israelites out of the increasingly oppressive hands of Rehoboam.

Why do you think the people of Israel called for Jeroboam?

They needed help from someone they could trust

The text does not explicitly say, but we can infer based on what we have read thus far that Jeroboam's noble and good standing with the people made him an ideal candidate to represent them and their concerns to Rehoboam.

Read 1 Kings 12:4. What did Jeroboam and the people of Israel ask Rehoboam to do?

lighten their labor load + we will serve you.

Read 1 Kings 12:6-15. What poor decision did Rehoboam make in response to this advice from the younger men?

he increased their word

Read 1 Kings 12:16-24. Rehoboam's decision set off a chain of events. What was the result for the kingdom?

he lost the kingdom + only kept 1 portion

It's in moments like this where we can start to wonder how God could ever bring good from such division. I love what Charles Spurgeon has to say about this,

> Notice also, dear friends, that God is in events which are produced by the sin and the stupidity of men. This breaking up of the kingdom of Solomon into two parts was the result of Solomon's sin and Rehoboam's folly; yet God was in it: 'This thing is from me, saith the Lord.' God had nothing to do with the sin or the folly, but in some way which we can never explain, in a mysterious way in which we are to believe without hesitation, God was in it all.[17]

How does this quote speak to you personally?

God is always w/ me even when I mess up

I know a lot has happened here so far. As a quick recap, fill out the chart below.

2
Solomon died, _____ established his kingship by calling all Israel together at Shechem. They summoned _____ from Egypt to take part.

(1 KINGS 11:43–12:3)

4
Rehoboam rejected the plea and abandoned the wisdom of _____ to take the foolish wisdom of his friends, the younger men, making the burden increasingly worse.

(1 KINGS 12:13-14)

1
_____ "lifted up his hand against the king," was persecuted by Solomon, and fled to _____.

(1 KINGS 11:26,40)

3
Jeroboam pled the case of the people and asked the new king _____ _____.

(1 KINGS 12:4)

5
The ten northern tribes rejected _____ as king and turned to _____ as their king.

(1 KINGS 12:20)

Imagine being Jeroboam in 1 Kings 12:20. He was now king over Israel! This was his opportunity to right the wrongs of those who came before him. The opportunity to really make a difference. To fight for and care for the people of God.

Look back at 1 Kings 11:38. What had God promised Jeroboam? What were the conditions?

Follow God, obey commands + He will rule over Isreal.

Keep these conditions in mind as you look toward tomorrow's study. Spoiler alert: I'm sad to say we're about to see Jeroboam deviate from being obedient to the Lord. Like I just mentioned, he had such a unique opportunity to help his people and lead them to follow the Lord. But instead of heeding the words of God, Jeroboam, out of fear, came up with his own plan. Not only did he deviate from God's instructions, he led his people astray as well.

This is a repeated pattern of these kings, these men of influence who had such an opportunity to do so much good. Somewhere deep inside of them, their motivations shifted away from God, and they led people astray.

This makes me take a step back and feel very challenged in the deeper motivations I have. Maybe we can dare to be honest together for a moment? No matter who we are and what our callings are, we influence other people.

Friends influence friends. Moms influence kids. Spouses influence each other. Our words influence those following us on social media. Big and small, we cause some sort of chain reaction with the influence we have.

> BIG AND SMALL, WE CAUSE SOME SORT OF CHAIN REACTION WITH THE INFLUENCE WE HAVE.

Take a moment and jot down some people you influence. You may have individuals or you may have spheres of influence. List whatever is applicable for you.

In light of this, I'm going to ask some challenging questions.

- Do we really want God's best for our finances, including tithing and giving to others, or do we have our own ideas about spending that prevent us from being generous? *yes, sometimes*

- Do we really want God's best for finding a spouse but then participate in activities that compromise biblical standards?

- Do we really want God's best for our job but then cut corners or try to get ahead in ways that damage our integrity and Christian witness?

- Do we really want God's best for our kids, or do we have our own plan for what a successful child is that distracts us from keeping God front and center in our family? ♡

- Do we say we want God's best for our marriage but then when God calls us to humbly apologize for saying something rude or harsh, we prefer to justify our actions and seek to prove ourselves right? ♡

- Do we say we use social media to encourage and help others but become so addicted to the affirmations people give us that we start posting more for personal affirmation?

- Do we say we want to lead a Bible study to help others learn about God but get completely offended when a friend goes to someone else's study rather than ours?

It's easy to start out with great intentions but over time have our real motivation get tainted. We develop a deep affinity for wanting what we want in the way we want it and in the timing we want it. We also have a deep affinity for shiny affirmations for our identity rather than just resting secure in our identity in Christ.

> Is there an activity or belief you hold that began with the right intentions but the motivation has become something else? Take some time to reflect and confess to God where your motivations have shifted. Ask for His help in realigning your heart and intentions in this area.

Here's the dangerous assumption: because our initial motivation is good, our motives will always stay pure. Sadly, that's just not the case. It's good to keep checking our motives and to be honest about our present intentions. Every choice we make has an internal motivation that's either pure or tainted. It's good to constantly check ourselves and be honest with what we see. Tainted motivations lead to misguided intentions that can lead to flat-out disobedience of God.

And one more thing to note: These kings received the blessing from God to be king and then their motivations seemed to get skewed. Paying attention to this, I want to look at the places where God has blessed me and see if the very things that should make me more trusting of Him are actually places where my distrust seems to kick in.

Again, please know I'm not at all pointing fingers here. I'm truly preaching to myself so I can do the heart check I believe this lesson calls for. And it's not to condemn but to course correct. We can all probably identify with some part of what caused these kings to struggle.

Ultimately, this is yet another opportunity to decide if we trust God or not. When we trust Him, we keep our motivations in line with His Word, His ways, and His instruction.

> Let's end today with writing an additional prayer. We already asked God for wisdom. Now let's commit to the Lord that we will personally apply His wisdom to our lives by being honest with our motivations and obedient to Him in how we live day to day.

THE FEAR *of* LOSING CONTROL

We distrust God when we are fearful of losing control.

When we try to take control, we ultimately leave no room for God to be God. We live in the harshness of the worst-case scenario, even though that probably isn't our reality at all. I do this all the time. I am triggered by a small fear, and instead of taming this thought, I feed it. I magnify it. I let it dictate my reaction. Everything gets blown way out of proportion because I convince myself that only my created protection will help me avoid the worst-case scenario.

When my daughter, Hope, was fifteen years old, she announced she wanted to spend her summer with a missionary family in a remote village in Ethiopia. The minute she told us what she wanted to do, my mind started racing through all the scenarios of dangerous possibilities, from her getting kidnapped to contracting a life-threatening illness where she wouldn't be able to get medical help to her plane crashing. Fear overwhelmed my emotions to the point that I couldn't hear any of the details she was sharing. I just quickly and sternly said, "Absolutely not!"

She kept trying to plead her case, but I shut her down and kept saying no.

I could see the hurt and confusion sitting heavy on her. And that look on her face kept popping into my mind over and over. I felt utterly conflicted. I wanted what was best for her but my fear kept overriding any consideration I had for letting her go. I wanted to protect her, but my desire turned into control the moment

I refused to pray and seek God about it. Any time I want my way more than seeking wisdom, I stop checking my desires with God and easily go astray.

Eventually, I felt God tugging at my heart with this thought: *The safest place for your daughter is in the center of God's will.*

Though I was still afraid and anxious, I slowly opened my heart to the possibility of her going on this trip. Now, granted, my fears were not unfounded. But as I released trying to control the situation, I gained a deeper sense of trusting God that if all the details worked out, I wouldn't let my fear hold Hope back from going.

THE SAFEST PLACE IS IN THE CENTER OF GOD'S WILL.

That summer missions trip did more to grow Hope's faith in God than anything else she'd ever experienced. God had a plan, and I'm so grateful my desire to control situations that make me afraid didn't derail that experience.

When have you done something similar, taking a concern and turning it into a big all-caps FEAR?

Many times

Instead of praying and seeking God, when have you ever tried to create solutions of your own making to ease your fear?

Jeroboam did this too.

Read 1 Kings 12:25-33. Why did Jeroboam not want the people to go to the temple?

He was afraid they would follow Rehobs + kill him.

He said he didn't want them to have to travel so far to worship. He made two golden calves for them to worship in Bethel and Dan. In reality, this was not necessarily to make things easier for the people. It was a created solution to help ease his fear. If he could keep the people from going to Jerusalem, he could keep them from potentially being wooed and wowed by Rehoboam and his way of ruling the people. Jeroboam was terrified of his people turning their hearts toward this other king and his own power being threatened.

> Have you ever feared losing the affection and respect of someone, whether in a friendship, a parenting relationship, a romantic relationship, or a working relationship? How did you react to your fear? *yes*

Jeroboam's reaction is a sign that he did not trust God. Instead, he led people away from going to the temple as God instructed. But, even worse, by placing the golden calves at the alternate worship sites he created, Jeroboam encouraged the completely dishonoring act of idol worship.

Again, before shaking my head at Jeroboam, I must challenge myself to consider where I might be doing the same thing. I'm not placing golden calves at alternate worship sites, but where might I be more concerned with protecting myself than remaining true to God's ways? For example, I know lying goes against what God's best is for me, but do I sometimes lie or stretch the truth to protect myself from the potential fallout of what telling the truth might cost me?

Or do I park my mind on a worst-case scenario and determine the only way to keep this from happening is to take things into my own hands? Do you ever do this too? Maybe you fear being single the rest of your life, so, instead of waiting for a godly man, you settle for a good man. He doesn't go to church and won't be able to process life with you from a biblical standpoint, but at least he's nice. You compromise to protect yourself from potentially living the rest of your life alone. Trusting God seems a bit risky, so you place your trust in a solution of your own making.

Or maybe it's tithing. You determine that your job feels a little uncertain and you know there will be extra expenses coming. So instead of continuing to trust God and keep tithing, you start to hold on to what's "yours" more and more. Doing this long enough will cause you to set your budget without room for the tithe. What was once something you saw as a visible way to trust God becomes an added burden you justify doing away with so you can protect the stability of your financial future.

> What have you taken into your own hands before? You probably didn't realize you were taking control at the time, but looking back what comes to mind?

I only point out these examples because, at different points in my life, I've struggled with them personally. And remember, we are choosing to examine the patterns of distrust we find in these ancient kings to make us more aware of places in our hearts where we are also distrusting God.

We do things all the time to protect ourselves. It's easy for us to justify an action for our protection. We may say it's for the benefit of other people when in reality it's our own manipulative attempt to control our situations and circumstances. We try to protect ourselves and keep things in our own control.

Jeroboam not trusting God not only led to his demise but also led the people astray from worshiping God as they were supposed to.

> Is there a place in your life where your need to control could be distracting or leading others astray?
>
> Trying to get kids to bed :")

The beginning of Jeroboam's demise can be traced to these political doubts. Jeroboam knew that a crucial aspect of the life of an Israelite was worship. However, in the midst of this divided kingdom, the temple of the Lord was in Jerusalem, in the Southern Kingdom. First Kings 12:26-27 gives us clear motivating factors for the doubt that crept its way into Jeroboam's life.

Doubt starts within the heart—"... and Jeroboam said in his heart ..." (v. 26).

> How often have you said things in your heart? What is on repeat in your heart?

High place where
Jeroboam worshiped

I've heard it said before that no one speaks to you more than yourself. Jeroboam was speaking to himself in this passage. In Jeroboam's case, the conversation revolving around worship tied directly to his political security and safety. First Kings 12:28 says Jeroboam took counsel that ultimately led him to a disastrous decision. This is an important reminder that the people around you are going to influence your decisions and provide either wisdom or folly. Scripture teaches us to surround ourselves with wise people from whom we can get good counsel (Prov. 12:15; 15:31-33).

Have you ever convinced yourself of something that turned out to be a mistake?

Could this mistake have been avoided by seeking wise counsel?

Who do you go to for counsel now? Why do you go to that particular person or group of people?

Dazzling Directors
Nick

Jeroboam feared the possibility that as the people of the Northern Kingdom traveled to Jerusalem to worship, they would turn their backs on him and return to the king of the south. Fear captivated his heart and led to doubting the promise of God. The fruit of Jeroboam's doubt and unwise counsel was the construction of the golden calves and the high places to provide an alternate place for the Northern Kingdom to worship. However, rather than building a temple for the Lord, Jeroboam reached back into the ancient past of the Israelites and constructed two golden calves.

Do the golden calves remind you of another story in Scripture? Turn to Exodus 32:1-7 and jot down all the similarities between the story there and the one we've been studying in 1 Kings 12:25-33.

Oftentimes, our sins are repetitive. Jeroboam didn't come up with anything new here. He looked at the repetitive sin of Israel and remanufactured it. He brought back the idols introduced to Israel by Aaron. In Exodus 32:4, in response to Aaron presenting the golden calf, the people said, "These are your gods, O Israel, who brought you up out of the land of Egypt!" Sound familiar? Earlier, we saw that Jeroboam reflected Moses in his act of liberation. Now, he reflects Aaron in his act of desecration of worship. Jeroboam justified his action by saying, "You have gone up to Jerusalem long enough" (1 Kings 12:28b). Jeroboam suggested there was a better place to worship than the place where God resided, the temple in Jerusalem.

What were the results of Jeroboam's actions according to 1 Kings 12:30?

It became a sin.

This one decision would be the undoing of Jeroboam as he led his people into sin.

Why do you think the people were so easily persuaded to worship these other gods?

*It was easier
The King told them to.*

Read Acts 17:11. Whether you are leading or being led, we are each responsible to know God's Word and to live it out. How are you examining your days using God's Word? In light of today's lesson, how does this challenge you personally?

Check the words/advice you're getting w/ scripture.

the PRACTICE of REMEMBERING

Like we learned yesterday, no one speaks to you more than you do. These conversations typically take place in the chambers of your heart and recesses of your mind. As we've seen, Jeroboam was led by fear that produced doubt in God's promise, which resulted in his self-deception and the sin of idolatry. But things did not have to turn out that way!

It's important to remember that Jeroboam was not processing his life on his own. He knew both God's law and commandments (the Torah) and also what God spoke to him personally about his future. All Jeroboam had to do was remember. Sadly, Jeroboam allowed his heart to manipulate his thoughts and fell prey to the temptation to take control of things himself.

Why is the practice of remembering crucial in obedience to God?

God's promise is forever

Take a moment and consider the depths of Jeroboam's doubts and how these thoughts of distrust rooted in his deceptive heart produced rebellious actions against God and manipulative actions toward others.

1. He set up alternative places of worship (Bethel and Dan) fearing the people would return to Rehoboam because the temple was in Jerusalem (1 Kings 12:26-30).

2. He made a temple on high places and appointed priests "from among all the people, who were not Levites" (1 Kings 12:31). (See 2 Chronicles 8:14 to understand how this was direct rebellion against God's commands.)

3. He appointed a feast "like the feast that was in Judah" (the Feast of Tabernacles) to compete with and draw people away from the feast that God commanded (1 Kings 12:32; 2 Chron. 8:13).

4. He changed the times of the Feast of Tabernacles festival to be exactly a month after the feast in Jerusalem.[18] This appeared to be so the people who would have been obedient to God and gone to Jerusalem to celebrate might come to Jeroboam's festival and be drawn in to his new religion, therefore remaining loyal to him as king (Lev. 23:34; 1 Kings 12:26-33).

What motivated Jeroboam to take these actions?
(See 1 Kings 12:26-28 for help.)

He was worried the ppl would turn to the other king — the heir of David.

What captivates your heart more often—selfish ambition or an ambition to make the name of Jesus famous? Fear or trust in God?

selfish
but I do want to follow God &
try to follow Golden Rule often I
think about making others feel important.

Whatever captivates our heart fuels our actions.

Remember, Jeroboam was never left to figure things out on his own.

> WHATEVER CAPTIVATES OUR HEART FUELS OUR ACTIONS.

Let's look at some verses where God clearly told Jeroboam of His plans to bless him and keep him safe, if only he would honor God and follow His ways.

Read 1 Kings 11:29-39 again. What reason did God give for dividing the kingdom of Israel? *Solomn's disobedience*

Let's not miss this important detail. Jeroboam knew the "why" behind the division! Jeroboam knew that any king who led God's people into idolatry would face consequences because idolatry was a sin against God.

Reflect back on 1 Kings 11:37-38—what is the promise God made? What did Jeroboam have to do in response to that promise? *God would bless his kingdom if Jeroboam would keep God's law & ways*

If only Jeroboam paused and returned to God's promise. Maybe the practice of remembering is something we need to implement in the areas where we find ourselves slipping in our trust of God. In fact, this type of remembrance is exactly what King Jesus requires of us, and why He calls us to celebrate communion, to take the bread and the drink "in remembrance" of Him (Luke 22:19).

What are some ways you practice remembering God's promises, whether in your church, in your family, or by yourself? *praying, affirmations scripture*

Remember in Day 3 when we discussed some things that may lead us to take matters into our own hands usually motivated by either fear, doubt, or desire for control? We can respond to our fear in faith based on what God's Word says. Read about these three motivations and then answer the following questions.

FEAR

The Bible is full of promises that help us not to fear, but that doesn't mean we'll never experience the emotion of being afraid. It's in those moments of being afraid that we have the opportunity to learn how to trust the Lord and rely on His Word. We know we can trust Him based on what Hebrews 2:14-15 tells us, "Since therefore the children share in flesh and blood, he himself likewise partook of the same things, that through death he might destroy the one who has the power of death, that is, the devil, and deliver all those who through fear of death were subject to lifelong slavery."

DOUBT

In the New Testament the theme of doubt deals with "man's dividedness of attitude when confronted with a promise of God."[19] (See Matt. 14:29-31.) We even see this in the Old Testament, "He is not afraid of bad news; his heart is firm, trusting in the LORD" (Ps. 112:7). We have no reason to live in this place of doubt and fear because God has given us His Spirit to empower us and fill us with faith.

CONTROL

We've already studied an example of control with Jeroboam. But we don't need to fall prey to the urge to take control of our lives because God is in total control and holds our very lives in His hands. Job 12:10 confirms this, "In his hand is the life of every living thing and the breath of all mankind."

Which of those three do you tend to lean toward the most—fear, doubt, or control? (And please know it's common to experience all three often!) *all of them*

Look up the following verses and jot down a few notes about each truth you can use to practice remembering when you return to fear, doubt, or the desire to take control.

Proverbs 29:25 Fear of man will prove to be a snare, but whoever trusts in the Lord is kept safe.

Romans 8:38-39 neither death nor life, neither angels nor demons, neither the present nor the future, ... will be able to separate us from the ♡ of God that is in Christ Jesus our Lord.

2 Timothy 1:7 For the spirit God gave us does not make us timid, but gives us power, love, + self-discipline.

2 Thessalonians 3:3 But the Lord is faithful, and he will strengthen you and protect you from the evil one.

For me, fear is what emerges first in my heart, which then tends to feed my doubts. Before I know it, I'm attempting to control things because sometimes I would rather trust in what I can do instead of placing my trust in God. Though the story about my daughter Hope from yesterday's study happened almost ten years ago, I think about that situation as other fears in my life emerge. Using God's truth and remembering His faithfulness from that experience has helped me fight fear in other circumstances. ♡

What is an example from your life where God's past faithfulness and His truth have helped you better handle your fear, doubt, or tendency to control? My car accident + recovery taught me God is in control and I don't need to worry about everything— I don't need to do it all.

Close today in prayer, thanking God for His faithfulness and His truth found in Scripture to help us remember we serve a trustworthy God.

THE END *of* THE STORY

If we stray from God's Word, we will stray from God Himself.

We may find ourselves in a place of disobedience we never thought we would be in. While we might not always intend to be disobedient, that's exactly what can happen when our hearts aren't being guided daily by truth.

I like to think of it this way: If I decide I want to stick with a healthy eating plan but I don't stock my pantry and fridge with healthy options, then when I get hungry and desperate to ease the ache I'm feeling, I'll go for something to ease my hunger pains quickly. And if the only things I have readily available are unhealthy options, I'll grab what's convenient. It's not that I intended to eat junk food that day—actually quite the opposite. I had the best intentions to be healthy. But all that went out the window when circumstances pressed in, my stomach started growling, and unhealthy options were the easiest solution.

Our souls crave to be filled just like our stomachs do. Our stomachs were made for food. Our souls were made to be nourished by God's Word. If we go too long without taking in the truth of God's Word, we will feel an ache. We may not realize it's an indication our soul is hungry, but the ache inside us gets more and more urgent. And since many options are readily available to give us relief, we grab for things that are in essence junk food for the soul.

> IF WE STRAY FROM GOD'S WORD, WE WILL STRAY FROM GOD HIMSELF.

What are some of those mind-numbing, falsely-satisfying, soul junk food options in your life?

busyness
scrolling social media
movies

We must start training our brains to recognize soul hunger. And instead of quick fixes that can lead us away from God and His truth, we must learn to recognize those desires for truth and learn to dig in for ourselves.

Over time, the more we read and study the Bible, the more we will learn and grow. God created our minds for logical comprehension and spiritual discernment through the power of the Holy Spirit. But even when we don't immediately understand what we are reading, we can rest assured that just the taking in of God's Word for ourselves will nourish deep places. Our souls were designed by God to receive and be nourished by the truth of God. We don't have to understand all the inner workings of our stomach for our body to be nourished by physical food; spiritual food is much the same.

> **OUR SOULS WERE DESIGNED BY GOD TO RECEIVE AND BE NOURISHED BY THE TRUTH OF GOD.**

Read John 14:26. Who helps you understand Scripture? *Holy Spirit*

There is one other thing to note. We must take the food in for ourselves—both physically and spiritually—in order for it to nourish us. Imagine being at a banquet and watching other people pile their plates high. You can smell their food. You can listen to them describe how wonderfully satisfying it is. You can see them take it in and get full. And this may make you curious about the food and want some of it for yourself. But you will not be nourished until you actually ingest and digest it for yourself. The same is true for Scripture. You must take in God's Word for yourself. That's why I often ask you to turn to read from the Bible. I want you to see the truth of Scripture in a personal way.

None of this is meant to evoke any kind of guilt. Trust me, I well remember the day I discovered the table of contents in my Bible with page numbers for the various books and felt a deep sense of relief that I could finally find the books of the Bible being referred to in church. Over time, I started to get a better sense of where different books of the Bible were, and I was able to connect the dots of the stories, timelines, and lessons about pursuing God's ways instead of my own feelings.

All of this is important for us to remember as we continue to look at the life of Jeroboam. The ruin of this ancient king started with his first actions led by the deception of his heart and not the truth and conviction of God's Word. That's the tragic lesson of Jeroboam's life and leadership.

In 1 Kings 12:30 we see how Jeroboam's actions impacted the people he ruled. Write the verse below in your own words.

He led ppl astray to worship idols + they went out of their way to do it.

The building of the golden calves was a sin that redirected the attention and worship of God's people from God to a false god.

When we take created things and give them value, worth, authority, and praise that only the Creator deserves, the Bible calls this idolatry.

What are some modern objects of idolatry in our culture today?

*Money   success
being liked
material possessions — home, car
influence*

Which of these do you see in your own life?

at times, all

No matter the idol, divided worship is destructive. From here on out we will see, repeatedly, the human kings lead the people of God into sin.

However, God did not sit by idly and allow His people to continue in the path of self-destruction. We can know God's goodness through the presence of His discipline and correction in His Word. In the Old Testament God's discipline often came through prophets He appointed. The Hebrew word used for *prophet* is **nabi'** and means "one who is called to speak."[20] Another common phrase used, especially in the Books of 1 and 2 Kings, is "man of God" (1 Kings 13:1). God used both a man of God and a prophet to bring correction and discipline to Jeroboam in light of his disobedience as a result of his wayward, distrustful heart.

Read 1 Kings 13.

A crucial connecting thread in Jeroboam's life is the way the "word of the LORD" continued to show up

Jot down how many times you see the phrase "the word of the LORD" in chapter 13. *alot*

I found "the word of the LORD" (ESV) ten times in this single chapter. Clearly, the word of the Lord holds significant prominence.

Let's dive deeper into the next chapter in Jeroboam's life.

Reflect back on verses 1-10 and answer the following questions.

What did the man of God do at the altar? *He declared it will be split apart*

What was Jeroboam's response and what happened to Jeroboam? *He tried to seize him but God shriveled his hand*

How did the Lord show mercy in this situation with Jeroboam? *He restored it.*

Jeroboam invited the man of God to have dinner with him, and though it would have been an honor to have dinner with the king, the man of God refused. Why? *God told him not to.*

Next, we read a somewhat bizarre story in 1 Kings 13:11-32. Do you notice any difference between the message given to the man of God and the message given to the old prophet? Make note of the messengers for each and the context given.

The man of God seemed to find himself in a tough spot. He had followed exactly what the Lord told him with Jeroboam and then was deceived by an old prophet. Did he really deserve the punishment he got?

You might be thinking, *This seems incredibly unfair.* Sometimes, when we approach God's Word we want answers to the why questions, we want things to make sense, and we want fairness to work the way we think it should. But maybe we just need humility today to lay down our questions for now. I might be one of only three people raising their hands in heaven asking about this crazy story. But let's reserve those questions for that day, not this day. Instead of expecting answers to why this story went in this direction, let's just approach this story with humility and a deeper desire to trust there's a reason this is in God's Word, and there's something we need to learn from it.

The "man of God" had very clear instruction given to him directly from the Lord! Notice how the old prophet lied and said, "An angel spoke to me by the word of the LORD" (v. 18).

> What is more reliable, the word of the Lord directly from the Lord or a secondhand message?

This is such a helpful reminder to ensure that we always seek firsthand information rather than settling for secondhand. Today, you and I can go directly to the firsthand source of all knowledge—God's Word and the indwelling Holy Spirit that leads us to truth. We must always check anything we learn secondhand against the truth of the firsthand information we have in Scripture. That's why it's so important to take in Scripture for yourself, like we talked about earlier.

Also, notice how the old prophet's false message told the man of God to do everything the Lord initially told him not to do! The man of God had every opportunity to go directly to the Lord to inquire of Him, but he chose not to. He chose to believe a message that was contrary to what God had already told him.

However, let's remember the good news for us today. As believers, we have the indwelling Holy Spirit, who is our Helper. He guides us into truth and illuminates the brilliance and depth of God's Word to us (John 16:13). So we have no need to fear God's Word. We can go directly to the Word and know the Spirit will help us as we study and pray. Remember, the man of God didn't struggle to understand God's Word here; he struggled to continue to obey it in the face of another option.

How does this story speak to you personally? Is there a situation in which you've heard or understood an instruction by God, and initially you obeyed it, but when faced with other options you didn't continue to walk in obedience?

We must always go back to God's Word to keep His truth front and center in our lives, especially as we make decisions. Again, I still have questions about the harshness of the consequences the man of God faced. But I don't want to miss what I do understand from this story because of what I can't understand in this story. So let's press on.

> ## WE MUST ALWAYS GO BACK TO GOD'S WORD TO KEEP HIS TRUTH FRONT AND CENTER IN OUR LIVES.

Let's finish today's study by reading the last two verses of 1 Kings 13, verses 33-34. How did Jeroboam respond to all of this in verse 33?

He didnt changed but appointed more priests in his idol worship.

I don't know about you, but verses 33-34 leave me wrestling. Why did Jeroboam not turn from his evil way? Why was his response to do the exact opposite of what he should have done to be obedient to God's Word? And why carry his sin so far as to ordain even more priests for the high places? I don't know these answers, but this is one of those places where I can personally challenge my tendencies.

Have you ever had a situation where you were confronted with something you did wrong and, instead of humbly admitting your wrongdoing, you justified your actions and then sought to normalize your behavior?

The more we justify and normalize a behavior in our lives, the less we feel a conviction that it's wrong. How does this resonate with you?

True

This is a tremendous reminder for us today to always turn to the Word of the Lord when we are in doubt. God has given us His Word as a gift to help inform us and as a means by which we can learn what it means to be conformed into the image of Christ. God's Word is shaping us to become more like Jesus; this is called sanctification.

Both the man of God and Jeroboam experienced God's discipline. They both fell short by not turning to God to guide their paths. They both were deceived. It would be easy for us to look at this discipline and question the goodness of God. It is so important to remember that God's justice is evidence of His goodness. In both of these instances we see the justice of God.

Why is the justice of God a good thing?

God always provides

As we end our study today, remember, we'll all have feelings of fear and doubt when difficult circumstances arise. What we do with those feelings matters. God designed our souls to be nourished, comforted, challenged, and corrected by His Word. Being filled up with His truth is what helps us overcome our fears and doubts. Then we are more free to experience His faithfulness and our trust in Him will grow.

Digging Deeper   GRAPPLING WITH TRAGEDY

For today's Digging Deeper, read 1 Kings 14.

There are some things I come across in the Bible that I just don't know what to do with. There are sections of Scripture that bump into a tender place in my heart, filled with grief and pain too raw for the words before me. First Kings 14 and the death of Jeroboam's child is one of these places. In order to study this chapter, I have to acknowledge the content is hard for me and refuse to personalize it or else I won't make it through it.

I personally know how devastating it can be to lose a child. When I was in my late teens, my baby sister, who was only sixteen months old, passed away after a liver transplant surgery. Though I was her sister, because of our age difference, I felt more like a second mother to Haley. And when she died, I grieved to the point where I wasn't sure I would ever get through losing her. It was such a dark season of my life. To this day, there are triggers than can bring flashes of that pain into my present circumstances.

If you are heartbroken by this kind of tragedy, I give you complete permission to skip this part.

But for those wanting to look into that which is hard to understand, God allowed this text to be included, and I guess I'm finally at a place of asking why.

It would be so easy to bypass this section. And I'm not saying looking into it is easy. It's extremely hard. One of the hardest realities in the Word is when I read about the death of a child that is tied to the disobedience of the parents. How do we wrestle through this "retribution theology" that doesn't apply in other passages of Scripture (in the case of Job and in the case of the blind man whose parents had done nothing to cause the blindness), but does seem to apply in this case and in the death of David and Bathsheba's child? Since we question it and wrestle with it in our hearts when we find it tucked within the pages of Scripture, here's something to consider.

HERE'S WHAT WE DON'T KNOW:

It is so difficult for us to wrap our minds around how death, especially how the death of a child, could be evidence of grace in any way. But we don't know what would have happened in the life of this child if he had lived as a part of the family of such an evil king. How would the impact of a culture and family bent away from God impact the outcome of this innocent child's life? What kind of king would this child become? We don't know what the outcome of this child's life would have been, but we do know throughout the long line of kings in both the Southern and Northern Kingdoms, the children of kings often followed in the footsteps of their fathers, doing even more evil in the sight of the Lord. Keep in mind, this is not an overall statement meant to be applied to those of us with hard realities in our family lineage, but it is a fact we are told regarding these kings. And it is a warning we can learn from.

Again, we don't know all the details but we do know that God was active in the midst of this story. What else do we know?

HERE'S WHAT WE DO KNOW:

We do know Jeroboam was making evil choices. He had done more evil than all who lived before him.

Jeroboam's evil actions stir God toward justice. Because of Jeroboam's sins, God spoke directly to the consequences that would be experienced, not only by Jeroboam but by his family and his people.

There is a compounding effect of Jeroboam's sin, culminating in the death of his son.

All of Israel would mourn this child.

His son would be the only one buried from the house of Jeroboam because he was the only one in whom the Lord found anything good (v. 13).[21]

> Don't miss the clue into a possible glimpse of God's grace—this child was the only one in the family that had good in him. In light of that, how might this fact be crucial in our consideration of these events?

HERE'S WHAT WE MUST CONSIDER AS A RESULT:

After six verses (1 Kings 14:7-12) of consequence of sin we are met in verse 13 with an incredibly unlikely and unexpected grace. God says, "For he only of Jeroboam shall come to the grave, because in him there is found something pleasing to the LORD the God of Israel" (1 Kings 14:13). God's action to allow the child to die peacefully and be buried is directly connected to seeing something pleasing in the child. God's tangible exercise of grace was the allowance of death and a proper burial.

It seems that the experience of God's grace is found in either a tangible or eternal way.

TANGIBLE:

We will experience God's unmerited favor in tangible ways in our lives on this side of eternity. These moments are gifts given that remind us of the goodness of the Giver of all gifts.

ETERNAL:

In other circumstances we may feel a void or unresponsiveness from God where His grace seems distant or even non-existent. In these moments we must remind ourselves that what we long for is actually already accomplished in the finished and victorious work of Christ on the cross. Therefore, we can be sure of experiencing what we long for in eternity with Christ.

VIDEO SESSION 3: JEROBOAM

WATCH VIDEO SESSION 3 AND RECORD YOUR NOTES BELOW.

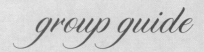

VIDEO GROUP DISCUSSION QUESTIONS

After watching the video, discuss the following questions in your group.

- How do you identify when you are departing from trusting God? What emotions do you experience as you move further and further away from trusting God?

- Where and to whom do you go to first when life is hard? How do you seek relief from painful or challenging circumstances?

- What did you learn about Jeroboam from this teaching session?

- How have you acted out of a desire to manipulate or control something?

- Where have you not been satisfied with God's timing and you find yourself navigating your own path?

- Lysa ends with the Lord's Prayer. What is the significance of the Lord's Prayer in your own life?

 To access the video teaching sessions, use the instructions in the back of your Bible study book.

Ahab and Jehoash

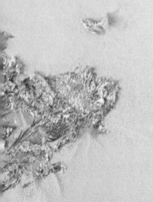

BUT AS FOR ME, I WILL LOOK
TO THE LORD;
I WILL WAIT FOR THE GOD OF
MY SALVATION;

MY GOD WILL HEAR ME.

MICAH 7:7

#TRUSTWORTHYSTUDY

Connecting the Kings

Between the kings we studied last week and the ones we'll focus on this week, five kings began and ended their reigns in the Northern Kingdom of Israel. The Israelite kings between Jeroboam and Ahab, whom we'll study this week, were said to have done "evil in the sight of the LORD" (1 Kings 15:26).

Their reigns were often short and ending in violence. King Zimri ruled for only seven days (1 Kings 16:15)! You can read more about their reigns in 1 Kings 15–17. You may recognize Ahab as the king often associated with Elijah and Elisha. These two prophets came to bring the word of the Lord in a dark time

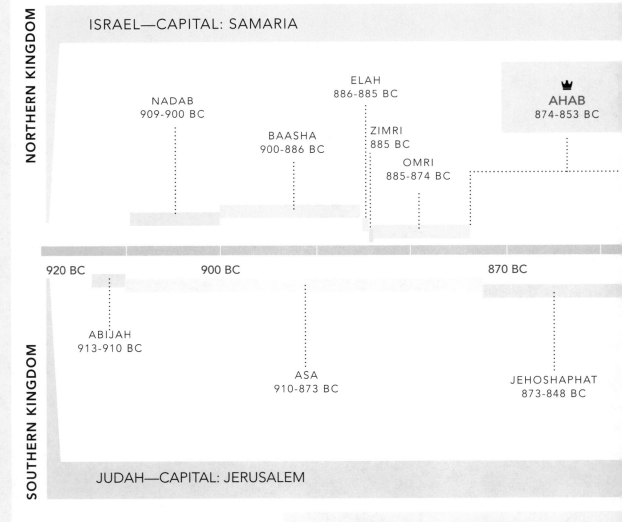

NORTHERN KINGDOM

ISRAEL—CAPITAL: SAMARIA

NADAB
909-900 BC

BAASHA
900-886 BC

ELAH
886-885 BC

ZIMRI
885 BC

OMRI
885-874 BC

♛
AHAB
874-853 BC

920 BC   900 BC   870 BC

ABIJAH
913-910 BC

ASA
910-873 BC

JEHOSHAPHAT
873-848 BC

SOUTHERN KINGDOM

JUDAH—CAPITAL: JERUSALEM

To study more about the kings, please see
the Guide to 1 & 2 Kings on page 207.

Please note: The dates listed are the approximate years each king reigned. Due to co-regency and other variables, these dates may vary by source.

in their nation's history, when their king was said to have been more evil than all those before him (1 Kings 16:30).

Meanwhile, in the Southern Kingdom of Judah, five kings (and one queen) reigned between Rehoboam and the king we'll hear more about this week, Jehoash. (For clarity's sake, please note that Jehoash is sometimes referred to as Joash.) The mix of rulers in Judah included both good and evil. You can read more about them in 1 Kings 15; 22 and 2 Kings 8–11. We'll discuss Jehoash's dramatic rise to the throne this week![22]

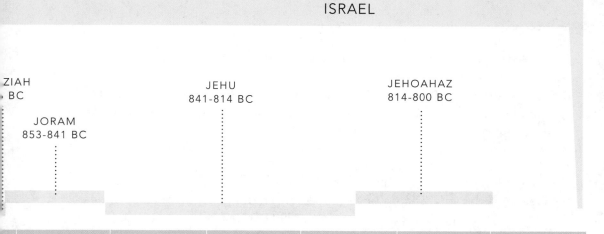

ISRAEL

ZIAH
BC

JORAM
853-841 BC

JEHU
841-814 BC

JEHOAHAZ
814-800 BC

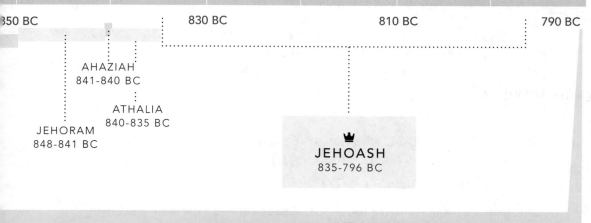

350 BC   830 BC   810 BC   790 BC

AHAZIAH
841-840 BC

ATHALIA
840-835 BC

JEHORAM
848-841 BC

♛
JEHOASH
835-796 BC

JUDAH

A TALE *of*
TWO KINGS

Ahab: King of Israel (Northern Kingdom) 874-853 BC[23] ·

Jehoash: King of Judah (Southern Kingdom) 835-796 BC[24]

Have you ever heard the saying, "When it rains it pours"? As we journey through the stories of these ancient kings of Israel and Judah it can feel this way. Each king seems to get progressively worse, and the people of God continue in a downward spiral. However, as we look closely we will come across a few kings who give us a glimpse of what a good king should be. This week we are studying two kings—one led the Northern Kingdom and the other the Southern Kingdom. These two kings led at different times (as you can see above), but we are studying them together this week to point out how they also led in dramatically different ways that produced different outcomes for God's people.

Read 1 Kings 15 and 16, paying close attention to 15:34; 16:2; 16:7; 16:19; 16:26; and 16:31. What is the phrase that's repeated over and over that lets us know history repeats itself unless the cycle is broken?

commited evil just as their ancestors

Look at 1 Kings 16:25-34. Who was Ahab's father? Look at verses 25-26. What kind of king was Ahab's father? *Omri - he was more evil than any before him.*

Did Ahab follow in his dad's footsteps? Check verse 33 for your answer. *yes — he was worse*

Ahab may sound familiar because he is often tied to the well-known prophet of God, Elijah.

> Reread verse 31. Whom did Ahab marry? What can we guess about his wife from this verse? *Jezebel — she worship idols.*

Ahab married Jezebel most likely early in the reign of Omri, his father, as a result of an alliance and treaty to provide economic and political stability. The result of this union was continued idolatry and worship of false gods. Ahab further established the worship of false gods for the people of Israel.

> Turn to Matthew 6:24. In this verse, we see the love of money as an example of a false god. How does worshiping anything other than the one true God usually turn out? *not good*

In Ahab's case, the worship of other gods ultimately (spoiler alert) led to the downfall of the Northern Kingdom of Israel.

Distorting God's goodness and His good gifts has been a goal of the enemy since he first slithered onto the scene in Genesis 3. We not only see this distortion played out in idol worship, but we also see it epically played out in the misplaced worship of God's beautiful gift of sex. So many kings struggled with this. But King Ahab's actions provoked the Lord's anger more than any king before him! His actions reflected a heart bent toward false gods and not the one true God. Ahab worked to erect a temple to house his altar to Baal in Samaria. As if this wasn't bad enough, Ahab also went on to build at least one Asherah pole and laid the foundation for many others to be constructed. Because he did this as the king, it made the building of these horrific places acceptable.

Asherah poles are alarming and, honestly, difficult to talk about. They were wooden poles that were named after the Canaanite goddess of fertility, Asherah.[25] They were placed where immense sexual immorality took place for a variety of reasons, all leading to further self-destruction and ultimately dishonoring God (1 Kings 14:15; 2 Kings 17:16; Jer. 17:2). It would be easy to think this was a "back then" problem. But make no mistake, the same demonic and tragic activities can be found in the casual sexual encounters today where people offer themselves without regard for their true value in God's eyes. And also in the horrific industries of sex trafficking and pornography.

The challenge here is when Christians, who are in covenant relationship with God, are also deviating from purity.

What are some subtle ways we fall prey to what's acceptable in culture in this area? *advertisments*

> JUST BECAUSE WE DON'T ALWAYS SEE GOD'S ACTIVITY DOESN'T MEAN THERE IS A LACK OF ACTIVITY.

Ahab and the people he led were slowly yet specifically breaking trust with God. They were choosing their own way and, in the process, rejecting God's way. However, God is too good to stand by and watch sexual sin and idolatry take place. This should remind us that, even today, God is not standing by and doing nothing with the sexual evils of right now. Just because we don't always see God's activity doesn't mean there is a lack of activity. Maybe if we can see God's activity in the context of Ahab, we can be reassured in the context of right now.

Read 1 Kings 16:32–17:7. How did God respond to the building of the altar for Baal and an Asherah pole? How would this have affected the people?

For the people of Israel, this drought would be devastating. It would disrupt and threaten every part of their lives. The irony about the lack of rain is that this is the very provision for which the people looked to the false god Baal. Baal (בעל, **ba'al**) was the Canaanite storm god and believed to be the bringer of rain. He was the chief of all the gods of Canaan.[26] Can you imagine what it would have been like for Ahab to hear these words from Elijah? It was a direct attack against the god he worshiped. For three years Ahab and his people experienced the drought. For three years we can imagine they must have cried out to Baal, the so-called god of the storm, to bring rain, but none came.

Can you relate? Have you ever relied on something other than God Himself only to find it lacking? How so?

The three years of drought could be viewed as punishment. However, we can also view it as a visible sign of God's grace as He lovingly called His people to return home to Him. The drought God established exposed the self-reliance of Ahab. In fact, the drought may have been a means of God's grace to cause Ahab and the people of Israel to turn from their wicked ways and back to the one true God, Yahweh. Sometimes we think of grace as being a covering for sin, but what if we look at grace here as God wooing the people back to Him?

How could this drought have actually been a way for God to rebuild trust with His people? *God shows them he is in control.*

How have you seen God lovingly call someone to turn from his or her self-reliance leading to sin and return to Him? How have you seen Him remind you to turn your heart back to Him?

As we look throughout Scripture we find that rain and drought were directly connected to covenant blessing and loyalty. Rain was the reward for covenant loyalty (*hesed*) and drought was the consequence for unfaithfulness (Lev. 26:4; Deut. 11:14,17; Amos 4:7).[27] The consequence of no rain was meant to call attention to their sin and raise awareness of their need to repent and return to the Lord. *Hesed* is not just a covenant loyalty but also steadfast love. Consequences are not just punishment but actually a loving way to redirect people.

Is there a place where God has allowed consequences in your life that you can now see as evidence of His steadfast love and need to redirect you? *yes*

Close today in prayer, confessing and asking forgiveness for anything you've been turning to for relief from your struggles instead of turning to God. Sometimes this means escaping our issues by numbing out or actively finding solutions of our own making instead of waiting and relying on God. However this plays out in your life, what is one change you can make right now to actively engage with God, seek Him, and turn your heart fully back to Him? Thank God for calling you back to Him. Praise Him for being the one true God.

DROUGHT
and DESPAIR

Even though we know that the drought was an act of God's grace to draw their hearts back to him, the people saw the drought as living in despair. And, unfortunately, living in despair for an extended period of time is fertile ground to grow distrust. This isn't a statement meant to evoke fear. Not at all. I simply want it to evoke awareness. The reality is most of us are walking through something hard that seems a bit too long. Or too unfair. Or too much for us to keep trusting God. I get it. I've been there. In those scenarios, I have to remind myself of previous experiences of God's faithfulness. Then I can borrow from those times of certainty for today's uncertainty.

> Remember what you already read in 1 Kings 17:1-7. Now read 1 Kings 17:8-16. Take note of how, even in this time of drought, God provided for Elijah, who was continuing to be obedient. How does this encourage you?

God will provide.

Living in disobedience and despair is where we find Ahab and the people who followed in his ways at this point in our study. For three years the Israelites experienced severe drought. Three long years of waiting, hoping, and praying for rain to return so that the people would not perish.

We discussed why the people of Israel were in this predicament yesterday.

> Look at 1 Kings 16:33–17:1 again. Why did God allow a drought in the land? *Ahab had idols + was doing more to make God angry than any other king.*

All the while King Ahab dug his heels in and ran further away from the Lord.

> Read 1 Kings 18:2-6. How did Ahab and Jezebel respond to the famine that resulted from the drought? *They were looking for any food to feld their livestock so they didn't have to kill them.*

It's interesting to see how Ahab responded to this drought in comparison to how King David responded to a three year drought in 2 Samuel 21:1-14. David's response was to seek the face of the Lord. King David dealt with the blood guilt of Saul, who murdered the Gibeonites. When David did so, his actions honored God and the Lord responded to the people's plea (2 Sam. 21:14b).

> How does this challenge you with your very next opportunity to respond to a hardship? *Turn to God.*

Now remember, it is a grace that over the course of three years the Israelites would come to terms with the inability of the false god Baal to bring rain. It is a grace that the people of God experienced pain and longed for rain because it placed them in a position to receive true grace and experience the fruit of blessing. Friends, this is a pivotal moment, a turning point for the people of God to return to the Lord.

In our moments of despair we often want to climb out of the pit ourselves and with our own strength. In 1 Kings 18:1 we see that the initiation and activation of this turning point is by the word of the Lord.

According to 1 Kings 18:1, what did Elijah need to do for God to send the rain? *present himself to Ahab.*

According to 1 Kings 18:17, what was Ahab's response when he saw Elijah? *accusing him of their problems.*

As a result of Ahab's reaction, a challenge was issued by Elijah.

As we just read in the text, the Lord told Elijah, "Go, show yourself to Ahab, and I will send rain upon the earth" (18:1). Don't miss the importance of this wording:

- Go,
- show yourself
- I
- will send

The passive participant in this story is clearly Elijah. It is God and God alone who provided the answer to the Israelites' cry for rain. God had a plan with a bigger vision in mind. It wasn't just about providing physical water for the people. It was also about providing a moment where the people could declare God as the one true God.

GOD HAD A PLAN WITH A BIGGER VISION IN MIND.

In John 4 there is a very familiar story about the Samaritan woman. I taught on this in my study *Finding I AM*.

Read John 4:7-15. What did the Samaritan woman want? What did she really need according to Jesus? *water* *living water – salvation*

What did the people at the time of Elijah in 1 Kings 18 want? *water*

What did the people really need that ran deeper than their need for physical water? *living water – salvation*

The same deeper encounter with God is what the Israelites needed in the story of Elijah. Now think about this in the context of your life.

> What spiritual provisions might God be working out in the midst of your cries for His help with a current problem in front you?

The people wanted rain. The woman wanted water. We want a solution to our problems. God wants to be the ultimate Provider of things we ask for and for the deeper spiritual needs we may not even be aware of. Our trust in Him grows when we look to His solutions being both what we want and what He sees we need.

> When have you seen God provide both a want and a need, perhaps in your life or in the life of someone you know?

God provided the opportunity for the Israelites to take action and declare their belief in the one true God. In 1 Kings 18:21 Elijah told the people they couldn't keep "limping between two different opinions." The Hebrew word for *opinions* is סעפים **(se'ippîm)** and can literally be translated as "crutch, which is used to support a weak leg."[28] The idea here is that the Israelites found themselves limping between Baal and Yahweh. The only stability they would find was the solid foundation of God. The word in Psalm 119:113 translated as "double-minded" comes from the same root word as *se'ippîm*.[29] "I hate the double-minded, but I love your law." Elijah was clearly letting the people know that the time of living "on the fence" was over. They had to determine who they would worship.

I think some of us can relate to the situation the Israelites were in. I often remind myself—and want to encourage you—not to place accusations against the Israelites without considering how we may react in

> OUR TRUST IN HIM GROWS WHEN WE LOOK TO HIS SOLUTIONS BEING BOTH WHAT WE WANT AND WHAT HE SEES WE NEED.

similar situations and circumstances. During this process I think we will find that we have more in common with Israel than we may want to admit.

For instance, in what ways have you found yourself on the fence in seeking wholehearted and faithful commitment to God?

Elijah reminded the Israelites that their real issue was not the death of rain for three years but the death of their covenant faithfulness (1 Kings 18:18).

Read 1 Kings 18:20-40. You may be familiar with this story, but read it with a fresh perspective, knowing the background a bit more.

How did the prophets of Baal prepare their altar and attempt to call down their god to burn the sacrifice?

He put wood + cut up calf

How did Elijah prepare the altar to the Lord?

He had 12 Stones, wood + soaked it.

What happened in verse 38?

God Burnt everything up.

YAWHEH, THE SELF-EXISTENT, ETERNALLY FAITHFUL ONE, IS GOD.

The turning point is fully realized in 1 Kings 18:39: "And when all the people saw it, they fell on their faces and said, 'The LORD he is God; the LORD, he is God.'"

No more doubts, distrust, or dependence on false gods. Yawheh, the self-existent, eternally faithful One, is God.

Let's end today in prayer, acknowledging that He is God. Ask Him to show you places where idols of self-reliance or any others are in the place that God should be.

PATTERNS *of* DISTRUST

I can know what is really true about another person by looking at their patterns. I don't say this to be negative but rather to be wise and aware.

When you've had a serious betrayal happen to you in a significant relationship you can go from being a very trusting person to someone you barely recognize, full of trust issues. It can be maddening trying to figure out how to heal and move on. Trust issues are complicated on so many levels.

One thing I've found especially helpful is a statement my counselor, Jim Cress, made to me: "Trust is built with time plus believable behavior." In other words, when you see a pattern of behavior that points toward healing and restoration, it builds trust. And over time, that believable behavior will rebuild trust.

But the opposite is also very true. A pattern of dishonesty will cause a severe erosion of trust.

Patterns are pointers. They can very much reveal where a person is headed. Their patterns today point to the way their future will play out tomorrow. We can't predict the future. But we can assess the future based on the fact that patterns point in the direction of outcomes.

Positive patterns tend to produce productive outcomes.

Negative patterns can't help but produce negative impact.

Obedient patterns tend to produce closeness with God.

Disobedient patterns can't help but produce chaos and destruction.

In Ahab's wife, Jezebel, we see a very alarming pattern of disobedience, false worship, negativity, control, jealousy, and selfishness. Her patterns had a direct effect on Ahab and show us clearly how those closest to us will impact us in either passive or active ways. The truth is, we are all either influencing others or being influenced by them. The question is whether those are positive or negative influences.

Take a second to list out those influencing you the most within your circle of friends, those you are close to, those who impact your actions.

Ask the Lord to help you see the ways they have influenced you in the past and write what comes to mind below. Maybe it's something small like buying a certain pair of shoes or maybe it's a bigger decision—where to live, where to go to church.

In what ways do you influence others?

In 1 Kings 16:31-33 we get in three verses the depth of the depravity of Ahab. Yet, we are not met with Ahab alone. We find that Ahab's marriage to Jezebel, the daughter of Ethbaal, king of the Sidonians, contributed to his wickedness. Notice how quickly Ahab built an altar for Baal. Sometimes I wish there were more details in Scripture to help us understand exactly how things came about. What was the conversation between Ahab and Jezebel? What we do know is that Jezebel worshiped Baal, and it is no small coincidence the first act recorded in Scripture after Ahab's marriage is the building of these altars. Passive influence is at play here. However, the influence of Jezebel quickly transitioned from passive influence to active influence.

Take a moment and read 1 Kings 21:1-16.

What did Ahab want to do with Naboth's land?

he wanted to plant vegetables.

What was Naboth's answer to Ahab's request?

No, God said NO.

Vineyard

Here are some cultural facts that may help you understand the story of Naboth on an even deeper level. Naboth refers to the land as "the inheritance of my fathers" (v. 3). It's important for us to see that the land was first given by God to his ancestors and this land was supposed to stay under the ownership of that tribal family (Lev. 25:23-24; Num. 26:1-12).

Read Genesis 12:1-3; Deuteronomy 12:8-10; and Joshua 11:23. List out everything you know about the land from these passages.

Land promised to Abraham
God promised land
Joshua took land and gave to ppl.

The land of Canaan was first given to Israel as a blessing and inheritance from the Lord. What Ahab was trying to do in taking away Naboth's vineyard is symbolic of a misuse of what's been entrusted to him. Ahab planned to misuse the land by taking it from the original caretaker, just as he misused his leadership of the people, turning them into idolatrous people.

I think we can all agree that what we find in 1 Kings 21:1-4 is an absolute royal pity party! But notice what happens with Jezebel. She had the opportunity to speak wisdom or wickedness. Jezebel actively influenced Ahab and led him further away from the Lord. Notice Ahab's response after Naboth's death (vv. 15-16). Scripture specifically says Jezebel told Ahab to "take possession" (v. 16) of the land and Ahab embraced the negative influence. The phrase "take possession" is translated from the Hebrew word **yāraš** and occurs ten times in 1 and 2 Kings, five of those instances happening in this very story (vv. 15,16,18,19,26).[30]

What does this repeated phrase tell you about whom Ahab and Jezebel worshiped? In whom did they trust?

Other gods beside our God

Has there been a situation in your life where you've attempted to "take possession"? What did your reaction to the situation reveal about your heart?

I think I need to control it.
Instead, I ~~should~~ can allow God to direct my path.

What Ahab and Jezebel (and many times we, too) failed to realize is that they lived under the sovereign reign and rule of the divine King of heaven. He is in control. He is the only One who can truly "take possession."

We will cover this more in the video teaching this week, but I want to draw your attention to a verse that reveals a lot about the dangerous influence Jezebel had over Ahab and the detrimental effect this had on Ahab's relationship with the Lord.

Write out 1 Kings 21:25.

There was never anyone like Ahab, who sold himself to do evil in the eyes of the Lord, urged on by Jezebel his wife.

Write out a prayer to the Lord, asking for eyes to see, discernment to realize, and courage to course correct from detrimental influences in your life. Ask God to help you be honest and to show you how to take God-honoring steps from here.

God help me to live in alignment w/ you — seeing the errors of my ways, repenting to you + asking forgiveness. Give me the ability ~~to~~ + strength to course correct + follow you. Help me to use my ears to hear you. Thank you for leading my path. I love you, God. ♡, Julia Amen.

JEHOASH'S CHILDHOOD

In stark contrast to Ahab is Jehoash, a seven-year-old boy who became the king of Judah (Southern Kingdom) through a series of unique and unpredictable events about twenty years after Ahab's reign in Israel. Your Bible may say Joash. His name can be spelled either way, but we'll spell it Jehoash here in the study.

Read 2 Kings 11:1-3 to find out about Jehoash's unique childhood.

We don't know a lot of specifics about his childhood, but we do know he grew up in the house of the Lord. Imagine living and being raised in a church building in a good way. Your world was getting ready for services, watching the preparation process of the teachings, gleaning from the deeper conversations around the Scriptures, and honoring the holy reverence of the environment around you. This was Jehoash's reality in the temple. But at the same time, imagine the heartbreak of watching the temple crumble because of being in a continual state of decline since the time of Solomon. As Israel continued to build altars and false places of worship to idols, resources were used for those purposes and the temple was neglected. It's not surprising, then, that one of the first things Jehoash did as king in chapter 12 was start the repair of the temple. If our beloved homes were falling apart and we had the resources to do so, we would probably be inclined to do the same.

Read 2 Kings 11:4-19 to learn about Jehoash's rise to the throne. I mean, drama, right?

I think it's safe to say that the loudest voices in the life of Jehoash were those he heard in the temple. Unlike Jezebel's influence on Ahab, Jehoash saw the patterns of worship, prayers, and time spent honoring and bringing glory to God. It's amazing to study Jehoash and connect his beliefs and actions to the crucial time he spent in the temple. He was surrounded by wise counsel and therefore incorporated wisdom more readily in his actions as a king.

We also see this in King David's life. Scripture teaches that King David, like many other contemporary kings, had counselors in his court (1 Chron. 27:32-33). His counselors' reputations and patterns of practicing wisdom spread amongst the ancient Near Eastern world.[31] Much of the wisdom we read about today in the Book of Proverbs came from the oral wisdom shared by these counselors to the kings. But remember, just because these kings had access to wise counselors doesn't mean they always listened to them or applied their wisdom. When they did, we see it played out in what they cared to tend to as kings.

If we are careful to apply godly wisdom to our lives, wisdom will lead us to care for the things of God.

IF WE REJECT GODLY WISDOM IN OUR LIFE, FOLLY WILL LEAD US TO BE FORGETFUL OF THE THINGS OF GOD.

If we reject godly wisdom in our lives, folly will lead us to be forgetful of the things of God.

This is true for the kings, and it's true for us as well.

Can you think of a time in your life when you've applied godly wisdom? Perhaps it came from God's Word or a trusted Christian friend or leader. What difference did godly wisdom make in how you lived your life during that time?

Now there's one more important detail tucked away in Jehoash's early years I don't want you to miss.

> Look back at 2 Kings 11:1-3. What did Jehosheba, Jehoash's tremendously brave aunt, do for him?

She hid him + his nurse

It's amazing, we never hear of this aunt again, but she is a true hero. Jehoash spent six years in the house of the Lord. Six years of watching, hearing, and experiencing all that took place in the temple. Six years of learning about the Lord in His house.

> Read 2 Kings 11:21–12:2. Who instructed Jehoash, and what influence do you think growing up in the temple had on his life?

Jehoiada the priest

Here's where I want to focus in the teaching today. Think about Jehosheba and how much it cost her to save her nephew: six years of her life holding this secret, fearing she and her nephew could get caught, and probably doing all she could to continue protecting him. But she still did her part in rescuing Jehoash. Then the priest did his part in instructing Jehoash. Then, in time, Jehoash could do his part repairing the temple and having people contribute to the repair, both with the money they were required to give to the priests and with offerings from their heart. Jehoash doing his part was crucial for God's people to do their part. All of this led to the people being given the opportunity to return to God as their true King. It wasn't a perfect process, and it took longer than Jehoash would have liked (we will look at this more in depth tomorrow), but both the repairs to the temple and the people turning their hearts back to God were significant accomplishments.

How does this personally motivate you to do your part? What is "your part" right now in this season of your life?

WE CAN TRUST GOD TO TAKE WHAT WE OFFER AND WEAVE IT INTO THE COLLECTIVE WHOLE WHICH MAKES A SIGNIFICANT IMPACT.

Each person doing his or her part led to a great good for God's people. Never underestimate how crucial your part is in any assignment with God. Whether it's tithing, taking a meal to help someone in need, serving in a ministry either up front or behind the scenes, standing up for godly principles in the workplace, or raising children at home—whatever our part is, we should always remember that no task is small or insignificant when we're on assignment by God. We can trust God to take what we offer and weave it into the collective whole, which makes a significant impact.

How has someone doing his or her part made an impact on your life and walk with Christ?

From what you know about Scripture and what we've studied so far, what do you think the temple represented?

Among other things, the temple represented the importance of wholehearted worship of God. As we studied earlier, Solomon, David's son, built the temple but made his own house even more extravagant. Jehoash took after David, the king after God's own heart. Jehoash sought to restore the outward brilliance of the temple as the people of God were drawn back to true, authentic, and wholehearted worship.

Isn't this pattern so interesting? David had the prophet Nathan, who spoke God's truth into his life. Jehoash had a priest named Jehoiada and the reality of temple life to speak into his life. Ahab had Jezebel, who spoke into his life, and, rather than repairing or rebuilding the temple of God, Ahab, through Jezebel's influence, built a house for a false god!

You may recognize a pattern of text exploration that I love to use when studying people in the Bible. I find it very helpful to list out both what we see and what we don't see in the Scriptures:

- What we know;

- What we don't know;

- What we can learn from this;

- What do I personally need to apply to my life?

The people around us can either lead us toward trusting God or lead us away from Him. We'll talk about this more in our next video. Take a moment to assess some of the kings we've talked about thus far and who influenced them most. Write the outcome of each situation in the space provided on the next page.

King	Influencer	Outcome
David	Nathan (2 Sam.12:1-15)	*David was convicted of his sin and repented.*
Solomon	Foreign wives (1 Kings 11:2-4)	
Rehoboam	Young counsel (1 Kings 12:6-20)	
Jeroboam	Counsel that constructed calves of gold (1 Kings 12:28-30)	
Ahab	Jezebel (1 Kings 21:25)	most evil king
Jehoash	Temple life, Jehoida (2 Kings 11:17–12:16)	repairing temple + bringing God's people back to God.

Remember, like we talked about with Ahab and Jezebel, patterns are pointers. And when we think about God's pattern, it points to His faithfulness, which is a reminder of how very trustworthy He really is.

To close today, read Psalm 78 and note evidence of God's faithfulness to the Israelites. Thank Him for being faithful and trustworthy today and forever.

REPAIRING
the TEMPLE

While Ahab worked toward the creation of a house for a false god, years later, we know Jehoash embarked on a project to repair the house of the Lord, the temple. Ahab placed his trust in the helpless hands of Baal, but Jehoash placed his trust in the more-than-able hands of Yawheh, the one true God. We see the devotion of Jehoash through his actions regarding the temple of God.

As we have studied before, the temple was the house of the Lord and the place where the presence of God dwelled. In fact, the ancient Israelites viewed the ark of the covenant inside the temple as being the "footstool" of God. They believed God ruled and reigned in the heavenly cosmos and extended His rule to earth by resting His feet on His footstool.[32] While this may sound a bit demeaning to call the ark of the covenant the footstool, it's anything but! This was the connection point between heaven and earth. This was where God physically touched our reality.

As tremendous and important as the temple was to the life and worship of the Israelites, like we studied yesterday, in the time of Jehoash the temple began to crumble. Today, I want to study in further detail why the temple was in such disrepair and the process of its restoration.

Second Chronicles 24:7 tells us that Athaliah and her sons began to break up the temple by sending objects from the temple to the altars of Baal.

Remember Athaliah? She was Jehoash's grandmother who tried to take the throne when his father (her son), Ahaziah, died. As pagan idol worship continued to expand, it directly impacted the temple.

> Put yourself in Jehoash's place, or in the place of any faithful Hebrew at the time. What emotions would you feel in connection to watching the temple be neglected?

> In what ways have you seen this same issue carried out today? I'm not talking about brick-and-mortar buildings necessarily, but where God's presence dwells. Read 1 Corinthians 6:19-20—what does this tell us about our bodies?

> Now, read 1 Corinthians 6:12-20 and list some ways in which believers neglect the temple today.

If I were Jehoash, the temple neglect would be a marked moment for me. It would be a constant reminder of all that was supposed to be yet was not. So when Jehoash became king, he set out to right all the wrongs he watched and observed growing up.

I know I've found myself in situations where I saw something was wrong. Things that just didn't settle well with me and left me with a choice to make: respond or run away. Jehoash responded in a godly way and it is a reminder for all of us to act in ways that bring honor and glory to God.

> Next, we're going to look at 2 Kings 12:4-16 together because, as you'll see, there's a lot going on here!

Jehoash repairing the temple was a sign and symbol for Israel and the nations surrounding them that God was in fact their object of worship. Jehoash's act of obedience to repair the temple reveals the good condition of his heart, a posture of love and adoration.

In the same way, our acts of obedience are indicators of not only our love and affection but also where our trust truly lies.

> Think through your reactions to your daily circumstances and hard situations in your life. What do they indicate you might be putting your trust in?

OUR ACTS OF OBEDIENCE ARE EVIDENCE OF WHERE OUR TRUST TRULY LIES.

Another important indicator of true trust is longevity and conviction. Follow-through is so important. It's interesting to note that the young King Jehoash initiated the repair of the temple soon after he became king (2 Kings 12:4). He gave clear instruction for how the work was to be funded and who was to be responsible, all under the guidance of the priest Jehoiada. But then, in verse 6 we find that by the time King Jehoash had reigned for twenty-three years, the repair had not been done!

> How would you have felt to know this task you cared about so deeply had not been done?

I think it's important to point out the reality that obvious trust issues would arise in a situation like this. Jehoash most likely believed Jehoiada could be trusted. We don't know what fell apart here. Was Jehoiada too old to do this job correctly? Was he greedy? Was he lazy? We don't know. But what we do know is how frustrating it is when you think you can trust someone to do something with excellence and they completely drop the ball.

> Have you had a situation like this in your life? How did you react?

Jehoash had a couple options. He could ignore the repair altogether because, after all his years as king, he had better things to do, more important affairs in the kingdom to handle. Or, he could get really angry and just punish everyone for not doing what he told them to do. However, Jehoash exhibited honorable yet just leadership. He went with a third option, holding the priests accountable, stepping in to change the process of how the money was to be received and used, and ensuring the work was done. After Jehoash instituted this new process, there was a complete shift in how the people trusted leadership. Let's not miss a small verse that could be easily overlooked, verse 15. Let's read it together:

> And they did not ask for an accounting from the men into whose hand they delivered the money to pay out to the workmen, for they dealt honestly.

Some of your Bibles may translate the Hebrew word for *honesty*, אמונה *(ĕmû·nāh)*, as "integrity" or "faithfully."[33] This word relays a sense of trustworthiness. I think it's important to note that Jehoash acted in an honorable and faithful manner as a leader to the people of God. And since people are often impacted either positively or negatively by their leaders, those who worked on the temple were honorable and filled with integrity in all they did in regard to the repairs.

The temple was supposed to be funded through:
1. Daily "sacred dues";
2. Poll-tax assessments of a half shekel for every registered male (Ex. 30:11-14; Matt. 17:24);
3. Payments taken for vows (Lev. 27:1-25);
4. Voluntary gifts or money given spontaneously from the generosity of the heart (Lev. 22:18-23; Deut. 16:10).[34]

I'm sure you know people of integrity, people you can trust. How do they display their integrity to let you know you can trust them?

Remember what we've been processing off and on throughout this whole study—trusting God. Do you see how the people's trust of giving to God increased when they saw they could trust the leaders who were managing the temple funds? How we handle our assignments from God and for God is important.

What is one way your integrity adds to or distracts from the people around you trusting God?

Read 2 Kings 12:17-21 to learn the rest of Jehoash's story. What happened to him?

> TRUSTING GOD MUST INVOLVE BOTH OUR ACTIONS AND OUR DEVOTION.

Unfortunately, under Jehoash's reign, the high places were still not removed (2 Kings 12:3). This is the sad conclusion to his story. Though he did seem to want to apply godly wisdom to his life and repair the temple, Jehoash did not tear down the altars to false gods, which were a distraction to the people wholeheartedly trusting God and led to devastating choices. (Read the disturbing account in 2 Chron. 24:20-27.) Trusting God is two-fold—we must trust that His wisdom is best and live accordingly, *and* we must constantly pursue removing all the distracting idols keeping us from wholehearted devotion. Trusting God must involve both our actions and our devotion. Remember, the Lord longs for a heart wholly fixed on Him.

Explain the difference between action and devotion.

Do you find it easier to trust God with your actions or your devotion? Why?

We know right actions are important. But right actions must stem from right devotion. A heart fully devoted to God produces right actions, not out of a legalistic stance or a moral obligation, but rather because God is the One our hearts worship, adore, and follow.

God is worthy of our trust. Today, let's declare God as trustworthy—the One who is the ultimate Provider, Healer, Restorer, Sustainer, and Holder of the best plans for our life.

As you close this week of study, pray, thanking God for His trustworthiness.

ALARMED AND RESOLVED AT THE VERY SAME TIME

One of my favorite kings to study over the last few years has been King Jehoshaphat. Although his story is only found in tucked away parts of Scripture, what I really love is how we can clearly see his absolute resolve to trust in the Lord.

King Jehoshaphat is mentioned in both 1 & 2 Kings, but there's also a unique story about this faithful king of Judah in 2 Chronicles 17–20. King Jehoshaphat was connected in alliance to the wicked King Ahab through the marriage of their children, so they ruled around the same time.

The political marriage of Jehoshaphat's son, the crown prince Jehoram, to Ahab's daughter Athaliah, cemented Jehoshaphat and Ahab's alliance (2 Kgs 8:16–18, 2 Chr 18:1). Ahab and Jehoshaphat's bond grew so strong that Jehoshaphat had a throne next to Ahab's in Samaria, Israel's capital at the time (2 Chr 18:9). Their alliance not only granted the two nations respite from conflict, but also allowed them to focus their energies elsewhere.[35]

We may question his decision to be connected to a wicked king like Ahab through marriage, but Scripture teaches us that Jehoshaphat was a good king who walked in the ways of David his father (sound familiar?) and did not seek after the Baals (2 Chron. 17:3). Rather than seeking false gods, Jehoshaphat sought after the Lord; therefore, God was with him (17:4). As we read Jehoshaphat's story we will come across a common theme that serves as an indication of the source of the king's trust.

Take a moment and read 2 Chronicles 17:3-4; 18:4; and 19:3. Look at some of the verbs used to describe how Jehoshaphat learned about God and His will.

As we study the life of Jehoshaphat, we will find that his resolve stemmed from seeking God.

For the sake of showing a clear connection between "resolve" and "seeking," take a look at 2 Chronicles 20:3. I love the NIV translation: "Alarmed, Jehoshaphat resolved to inquire of the Lord, and he proclaimed a fast for all Judah."

Do you see how King Jehoshaphat's name is bookended in two realities: alarmed and resolved? He had both the feelings of alarm that are a natural human response to his threatening situation and a supernatural resolve to inquire of the Lord. The resolve was a predetermined pattern built over time that emerged as naturally as the feelings of alarm rose within him.

I want this for my life. I want my resolve to inquire of the Lord to be my first response, not my last resort when feelings of alarm arise with threatening situations. But to be honest with you, I think I still need some work in this area. When I get caught off guard, stunned by threatening circumstances, or unexpectedly wounded by a hurtful statement, I can literally feel my body being overrun with a flood of emotions. Based on conversations with different friends of mine with different personalities, it seems like each of us has a go-to feeling that rises up and wants to take over in threatening situations—anger that wants to come out swinging, fear that wants to shrink back and disappear, confusion that wants to talk it out and restore peace quickly, just to name a few.

Though seeking the Lord doesn't always come naturally as my first response, it is the only way to infuse supernatural strength into my resolve. The more I turn to the Lord in daily struggles, the more natural it is to return to Him in times of unexpected trouble.

One of my favorite passages within the theme of seeking is an important topic and phrase in the narrative of Jehoshaphat, as we've seen in the Scriptures we have just studied. The Hebrew word translated as "seek" or "inquire" is דרש (dā·răsh).[36] In the story of Jehoshaphat it has a basic meaning of worship (2 Chron. 1:5; 15:12). The reason for his resolve was a higher trust in God than all of his military might, riches, and political alliances.

How was it possible for Jehoshaphat to have such strong resolve? Do you see how important preparation before the time of trouble hits is key to having a resolved response when it does?

One of the most powerful moments in the life of Jehoshaphat is when he led his people to seek after the Lord (2 Chron. 20:3-5). King Jehoshaphat stood up among his people and declared some very important truths about God. These are truths that you and I must rehearse to ourselves with regularity because they will reorient our wayward hearts to return and seek the Lord.

> Take a moment to read King Jehoshaphat's prayer, and identify the various truths about God in 2 Chronicles 20:6-12.

I love 2 Chronicles 20:21, an easily overlooked detail of King Jehoshaphat's leadership. Notice that he "had taken counsel" with the people. You may recall King Rehoboam (1 Kings 12), who followed negative council that ultimately led to the division of the kingdom. But King Jehoshaphat took wise counsel and appointed "those who were to sing to the Lord and praise him in holy attire, as they went before the army, and say, 'Give thanks to the LORD for his *steadfast love* endures forever'" (2 Chron. 20:21, *emphasis mine*). Jehoshaphat and the singers underscored steadfast love as a characteristic of God. In connection to the powerful prayer recollecting the truth about God, the Israelites were remembering the covenant love of God. The Hebrew word translated here as "steadfast love" is חסד *(ḥĕ·sĕḏ)* and refers to an unfailing love that is based on covenant commitment, promise, and relationship.[37] In other words, the Israelites could be confident going into battle, not because of what they could muster up in terms of their own strength, but because of the mighty hand of their covenant-keeping and faithful God.

> Read 2 Chronicles 20:22-24. It's an amazing ending to this story. Recall all the many ways King Jehoshaphat honored God and note how God fought for them.

Instead of lifting up human weapons, they lifted up praises to their God and their enemies were defeated. Lastly, read the long-lasting effect this had on Jehoshaphat and his kingdom in verses 29-30. There was peace and rest.

Now, there is a verse we must not skip over that points out a repetitive sin present in the reigns of many good kings. Verse 33 says, "The high places, however, were not taken away; the people had not yet set their hearts upon the God of their fathers."

While it is amazing to pause and reflect on a king like Jehoshaphat—a good king who turned to the Lord—it is important to note the "however" of his life. This challenges me to search my heart and life for any "however" that may exist.

VIDEO SESSION 4: AHAB

WATCH VIDEO SESSION 4 AND RECORD YOUR NOTES BELOW.

God is good.
He ultimately wins the battle against sin.
Knowing this, I can trust him.

VIDEO GROUP DISCUSSION QUESTIONS

After watching the video, discuss the following questions in your group.

- How familiar are you with the biblical term *armageddon*? Why is it important to understand this location?

- How do your feelings continue to influence your trust in God?

- Who are the people around you who influence your trust in God?

- Lysa asks three questions in the video teaching. Discuss your answers as a group.

  1. Is there anyone in your life who influences you to justify thoughts and actions that go against God's Word?

  2. Are there some people in your life you regularly allow access to help you check what you're thinking and doing to make sure it's in line with God's Word?

  3. If there are wise people speaking out cautions to you, are you willing to listen and redirect your actions?

- What are ways you can encourage one another to look to Jesus and God's Word, the Bible, as you remember that "God is good at being God, so we can trust Him"?

 **To access the video teaching sessions,** use the instructions in the back of your Bible study book.

123

Hezekiah

EVERY WORD OF GOD PROVES TRUE; HE IS A SHIELD TO THOSE WHO TAKE REFUGE IN HIM.

PROVERBS 30:5

#TRUSTWORTHYSTUDY

Connecting the Kings

Between the last kings we studied and this week's focus, a lot happened in the ancient world! Israel went through twelve more kings (most of them evil) before being captured by the Assyrians around 722 BC. You can read all about their stories in 1 Kings 22; 2 Kings 1–3; 9–10; 13–15; and 17. Some of the prophets you may be familiar with—Elisha, Amos, Hosea, and Jonah—lived and preached during the reigns of those kings, often warning them of the captivity that was coming for them.

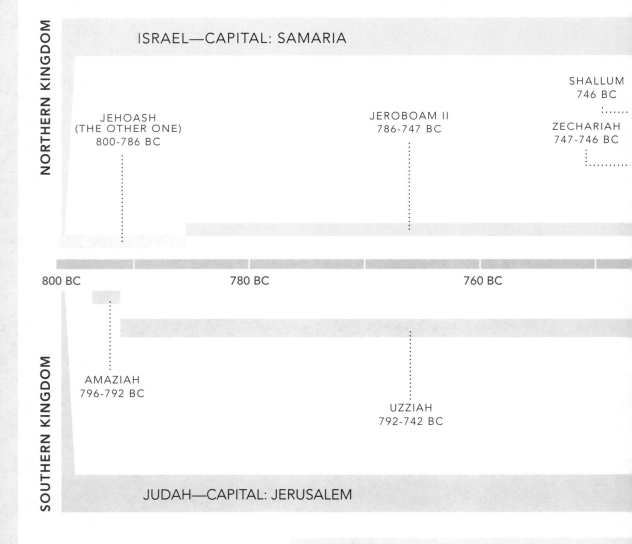

NORTHERN KINGDOM

ISRAEL—CAPITAL: SAMARIA

JEHOASH
(THE OTHER ONE)
800-786 BC

JEROBOAM II
786-747 BC

SHALLUM
746 BC

ZECHARIAH
747-746 BC

800 BC   780 BC   760 BC

SOUTHERN KINGDOM

AMAZIAH
796-792 BC

UZZIAH
792-742 BC

JUDAH—CAPITAL: JERUSALEM

To study more about the kings, please see the Guide to 1 & 2 Kings on page 207.

Please note: The dates listed are the approximate years each king reigned. Due to co-regency and other variables, these dates may vary by source.

Over in Judah, four kings reigned between Jehoash and Hezekiah whom we'll study this week. They were a mix of good and evil, often beginning with the best intentions, but as we've seen so often in our study, being led astray to trust in anything other than the one true God. You can read more about their reigns in 2 Kings 14–16. This week we'll dive into Hezekiah's story.[38]

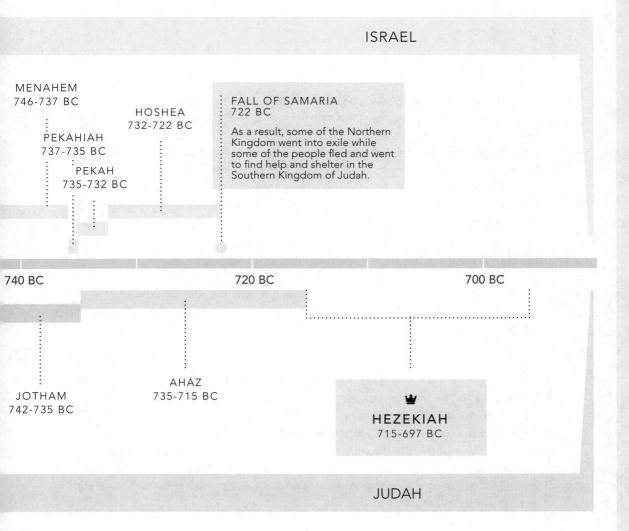

ISRAEL

MENAHEM
746-737 BC

PEKAHIAH
737-735 BC

PEKAH
735-732 BC

HOSHEA
732-722 BC

FALL OF SAMARIA
722 BC

As a result, some of the Northern Kingdom went into exile while some of the people fled and went to find help and shelter in the Southern Kingdom of Judah.

740 BC   720 BC   700 BC

JOTHAM
742-735 BC

AHAZ
735-715 BC

♛
HEZEKIAH
715-697 BC

JUDAH

A KING
of TRUST

I want to trust God until I don't.

In my book *It's Not Supposed to Be This Way*, I stated my tension with fully trusting God this way: "When God's promises seem doubtful, when His timing seems questionable, and His lack of intervention hurtful," when I see God answering other people's prayer requests in the exact way I've begged Him to answer me but hasn't yet, it feels like a form of divine rejection.[39] When I see other people's trials turn into triumph quickly, it makes my places of long-suffering feel even more unbearable. God's timing for me starts to feel incredibly unfair. And when I know He is powerful enough to change those hurting me, fix my circumstances, and intervene as my great Defender, and yet He doesn't seem to be doing any of that, it messes with me.

> Though we've made a lot of progress in this study, do you still sometimes doubt that God is actually going to come through for you personally?

When I struggle with doubting that God is trustworthy, it isn't in the global sense. I know He's trustworthy in general—I just wonder if He's going to come through for me personally. When this happens, it makes me want to rally more of my own strength rather than rely on God's strength. Before I even know it, I say I trust God with my mouth, but in reality I get overwhelmed trying to fix and control things myself. I get stressed out, overly emotional, and more and more distant from God. My trust in God becomes nothing but a statement I feel I should say but not what I'm actually living out.

Distrust has settled in.

Self-reliance has become my go-to.

And I wonder why the world feels scarier than ever, I feel more and more exhausted, and circumstances seem absolutely impossible. Hope slips away. Redemption seems like a pipe dream. Trust becomes something better Christians with holy lives can do, but not me.

I don't run to worship false gods on the high places. I don't have to. I have my own high place. I rely on myself and solutions of my own making above trusting God. And when you get right down to it, isn't that very much the same as what we see the Israelites doing when they worship the false gods of their own making as well?

Yikes. Please hear me, it's as hard for me to type those words as it is for you to read them. But honest admission is the first step to climbing down from the high places and into the compassionate arms of God, where hope stirs inside me once again.

That sounds like a good thing to do at this point of our study, but how? This can't just be a message that preaches well in theory with no way to live it out practically.

> Take a moment and pray that God will show you the idols in your own life. Ask that you will be able to step into hope and forgiveness as He shows them to you.

Well, the king we will study this week finally shows us how. King Hezekiah was the unfortunate recipient of years of the patterned practice of high places. But he was the one who finally obeyed God's command to remove the places of false worship and showed us what it looks like to step away from the high places and toward truly trusting God.

But let's first start with the condition of the Israelite people before King Hezekiah began his reign.

At this point in our study it may seem like there is absolutely no hope for the people of God. We have clearly seen what takes place when distrust settles in and corruption creeps into the lives of the previous ancient kings of Israel. Theologian T. Desmond Alexander unpacks the incompatibility of corrupt human kingship with the divine King by saying,

> Corrupted human kingship is about taking possession of the earth and using power to control others. Divinely instituted kingship is quite different. It seeks to re-establish God's sovereignty on the earth in line with the divine mandate given to human beings when first created. Because these two forms of kingship are mutually incompatible, they naturally come into conflict.[40]

I know the above quote contains deep thoughts, but this is worth considering. These two forms of kingship are so different because a human king's imperfections stand out so clearly against God's perfection. Human kingship is about self-preservation and possession using humanity to bring glory to self. God's kingship is selfless preservation for humanity multiplying God's glory through the earth.

Read Genesis 1:27-28. What was the divine mandate given to human beings when first created?

Be fruitful + rule over everything in the earth.

I think we could pause here and take a moment to really consider what was happening with God's divine mandate to Adam and Eve. It's important for us to understand this mandate because it was what God expected the kings of Israel to continue to follow through on. The divine King gives His children the responsibility to not only bear His image but to multiply, be fruitful, and take dominion. Something that can be overlooked is what actually happens during the multiplication and dominion.

What do you think it means when God commanded His people to be fruitful and multiply?

have more kids + continue those values

Because all people are made in the image of God, we reflect His brilliant glory. As Adam and Eve were supposed to multiply and be fruitful, in essence they were to spread the brilliant glory of God throughout the earth. After the fall, God did not give up on His divine will for the earth to be filled with His glory (Num. 14:21; Ps. 72:19). This is why the very command we have been given as Christ followers is to make disciples of all nations (Matt. 28:19). Because we are made in the image of God, when we make disciples, we are spreading the glory of God across the earth.

Instead of reflecting God's glory, many of the kings of Israel reflected corrupt kingship where their pursuit was to leverage their own means to take possession of the earth for their own gain. However, in 2 Kings 18 we meet Hezekiah, the king of Judah, an unexpected heroic king who did quite the opposite. Hezekiah began his reign when he was just twenty-five years old.

> I think it's so important to read the actual words of the Lord, so before we go any further, take a moment to read 2 Kings 18:1-4 and write down everything about Hezekiah that stands out to you.

25 yrs old
29 yr reign

He did what was right in eyes of the Lord, removed high places, smashed sacred stones + cut down the Asherah poles.

Hezekiah, just like his ancestor King David, did what was right in the eyes of the Lord. But then in verse 5 we see exactly what set Hezekiah apart from the other kings:

> He trusted in the LORD, the God of Israel, so that there was none like him among all the kings of Judah after him, nor among those who were before him.

Trust. Hezekiah was a king who put his trust and faith in the divine King. Hezekiah lived his life (for the most part) from a place of dependence on God rather than depending on himself. This fact separated Hezekiah from every other king who came before him and would come after him. We've been tracing the theme of trust throughout our study of Kings. We've seen specifically how often distrust was on display amongst many of the kings. Here in 2 Kings 18:5 we find a clear indication of a king who placed his trust in the Lord.

The Hebrew word בטח (bāṭaḥ) translated as "trusted" in this verse, occurs several times in Kings.[41]

Let's look at these verses and see where Hezekiah's trust could have been placed.

Verse	Options for Hezekiah's Trust
2 Kings 18:5-6	Hezekiah trusts the Lord and His commandments.
2 Kings 18:19-20a	Hezekiah could trust in words as strategy or power for war.
2 Kings 18:20b-21	Hezekiah could trust in Egypt/Pharaoh.
2 Kings 18:22	Hezekiah trusts in the Lord.
2 Kings 18:24	Hezekiah could trust in Egypt for its chariots and horsemen.
2 Kings 18:30	Hezekiah trusts in the Lord who could deliver them.
2 Kings 19:10	Hezekiah trusts in the Lord.

Did you notice a pattern? What does that tell you about Hezekiah?

Hee trusted in The Lord
even in time of uncertainty

Though Hezekiah could have trusted in those other things in each situation, he kept trusting God. It's interesting that the Lord says through the prophet Isaiah, "Behold, I will put a spirit in him [King of Assyria] so that he shall hear a rumor and return to his own land, and I will make him fall by the sword in his own land" (2 Kings 19:7). In other words, the only strategy that would work to defeat the King of Assyria is God's strategy. So only by trusting God would Hezekiah be able to defeat the King of Assyria. All the other things mentioned in the chart would have never accomplished what only God could accomplish.

How does Hezekiah's trust speak to a situation you are in and your decision to choose to trust God or rely on other things?

God's way is better

As we've progressed through this study, we've had the benefit of looking at the Israelites' distrust. But today I want us to also look at ourselves. The following questions may be difficult to answer, but ask God to help you be honest, knowing there is forgiveness and hope and freedom in the One worthy of our trust.

Where are you with trusting God?

I can trust + then get distracted

Are there situations in your life where trusting God seems harder than others? Why do you think that is?

What is one thing you've learned about trusting God that you've found helpful in your harder circumstances?

Close this day's study in prayer, thanking God for the example of Hezekiah. Thank God for being the One who is worthy of all our trust and all the glory.

the TEST of TRUST

Do you ever look around at all that is happening in our world today, or even within the realm of your own life, and feel fear grip your heart?

I think it's a feeling we have all faced at some point in our lives. We crave safety and certainty and simplicity as we raise our families, serve God, and live out our Christian beliefs in both private and public. But so many things feel threatening to those desires.[42]

Nothing tests our trust like fear, but fear fades when we trust the strength and sovereignty of our God. We touched on this a bit in Week 2, but since fear is such a driving force that feeds distrust and is a common human experience, I want to spend some more time here. Not only that, but the text today demands it.

Fear has a way of crippling us and taking us from confidence into conflict. We find ourselves in conflict because we begin to doubt the very things we thought we could trust. In 2 Kings 18:13-37, the great king Hezekiah, who had placed all his trust in the Lord, was tested.

> Take a moment to read 2 Kings 18:13-16. Turn to 2 Chronicles 32:1-8 and read more about this incident.

Taking those two sections of Scripture, along with what you know about human nature, how do you think Hezekiah felt when he learned the Assyrians were planning to attack Judah?

He was unsure

NOTHING TESTS OUR TRUST LIKE FEAR.

How do you think the people felt? What clue does 2 Chronicles 32:7-8 give you about the feelings of both Hezekiah and the people?

They trusted in God + they felt confident God would protect them.

This had to be a scary situation for the people of Judah and for Hezekiah himself. While Scripture says that he trusted in God, we are not sure what caused him to give the treasures of the temple. Perhaps it was part military strategy—the temple most likely held the most valuable objects in the kingdom. Hezekiah might have thought a bribe would appease the oncoming army and his people might be spared. Perhaps, though, Hezekiah had a momentary lapse in trust. We can see how that would happen, right? Whenever an attack comes our way, whether that attack is illness, financial trouble, relationship issues, or an Assyrian army, we tend to forget who our God is, even momentarily. Perhaps we try to take matters into our own hands first, grasping for anything to hold off the war that is coming.

We don't know from Scripture that this is how Hezekiah felt, but I know it is how I would have felt.

How do you typically react at first when an attack comes your way?

Try to do things my way

Ask the Holy Spirit to illuminate your own fears that can cause similar knee-jerk reactions.

This is honestly refreshing for me to see. It wasn't Hezekiah's perfection that helped him step into deeper trust with God; it was his humble heart in the midst of the same kinds of human fears that you and I experience.

Read 2 Kings 18:17-19.

When our trust is tested by fear we are forced to question everything we believe in. The enemy is waiting like a hungry lion to pounce on this opportunity to question, disillusion, and cause us ultimately to distrust the Lord. Notice the direct message of the king of Assyria through Rabshakeh: "Thus says the great king, the king of Assyria: On what do you rest this trust of yours?" (v. 19).

I think this is the question that plagues our hearts every moment our trust in the Lord is tested. On what do we rest our trust? In whom do we trust?

As we look back at King Hezekiah's story we find initial wholehearted trust in the Lord. When pressed by the Assyrian army, he took the gold and silver from the house of the Lord, believing it would appease the Assyrian king and rescue them from attack and defeat.

But things did not go as Hezekiah had hoped. The retreat of the Assyrian army was short-lived, and the tribute ultimately failed him. As you read through 2 Kings 18:17-19, you'll see another aggressive act by the Assyrian king—he sent a messenger to Hezekiah with a threatening message for all around him to hear.

Who was the messenger, with whom was he traveling, and where was this announcement being made?

Supreme commander / chief officer & field commander w/ large army

water

Let's clarify who was being sent with this message of fear from the king of Assyria to Hezekiah's men and his court. Your Bible might say the king of Assyria sent his supreme commander, chief officer, and field commander with a large army. The ESV says he sent the Tartan, the Rab-saris, and the Rabshakeh with a great army. Just so you can better understand, these were high-ranking officials sent as royal messengers from the Assyrian king.

Read 2 Kings 18:19-27. Notice the strategic approach of the Assyrian king to cause the people to distrust and stop depending on the Lord. Whom did he accuse Hezekiah of trusting in? (There are two answers.)

Egypt + God

The Assyrians often attacked the deities of other kingdoms as a war strategy, telling the people their god was angry with them for a variety of reasons. So it's not a surprise they would try this tactic with Judah.[43] It's also interesting to note that the original Hebrew shows Rabshakeh went from speaking directly to Hezekiah (through his men) to speaking to the crowd.[44] This was a very specific and crafty strategy. Rabshakeh was using this opportunity to include all the people who could overhear the conversation to incite doubt in Hezekiah and ultimately distrust of God.

But also see the correlation here to what our enemy uses to tempt us to distrust God. The temptation is usually just a counterfeit promise that causes us to doubt the perfect promise of the Lord.

In verse 26, what does Eliakim ask of the Assyrians? Why do you think he asked this?

Speak in language only the officials know — not what commoners know.

Like I said, as we look closely at the story, we find that the conversation is not just happening between the servants of the Assyrian king and Hezekiah but in front of those who were on the walls! Eliakim asked for the Assyrians to speak in Aramaic and not in the native language of the Judeans in fear that they might hear all that was taking place. The response is clear—the message of fear was for all, including those sitting on the wall listening (v. 27).

The Assyrian messengers' strategy was specific and calculated.

First, the messengers caused the people to question their trust in God as their deliverer. Second, the Assyrian king, who called himself "the great king" (v. 19), offered the people of God a counterfeit promised land. All they needed to do was turn from trusting in the Lord to trusting him. The Assyrian king claimed to be the only true deliverer who could save the people.

Read 2 Kings 18:32 and compare it with Deuteronomy 8:7-9.

Land of milk + honey promised land

When have you been tempted with similar counterfeit promises?

freedom when I stay up late.

What can you do now to help you overcome these temptations when doubts arrive?

trust in God's design of night & day.

Tomorrow we will see what Hezekiah did and the wisdom the prophet Isaiah shared for the situation. But here's my big lesson today: I need to remember the enemy is vicious, but he is not victorious. Therefore, I can sometimes feel afraid, but I don't have to live afraid. And even more importantly I can remember that fear doesn't have to pull me away from trusting God. Fear can actually be the catalyst to me choosing to trust God more than ever.[45]

TRUSTING *the* DELIVERER

Today we are faced with promises of deliverance and rescue at every turn. These deliverers present themselves to us on social media, in our workplaces, and in our homes. They promise to provide for us, and that's not bad—until it is. It's easy for a line to be crossed where, in the name of provision, we start chasing a vision that can subtly and simultaneously weaken our trust and faith in God.

Please don't start your mind down a path of other people who are doing this. I'm not pointing out a person. I'm simply reminding myself to be more aware of my need for the one true Deliverer and aware of the potential distractions promising a shadow version of delivery.

Social media will tell you, "Here's how you can be the better version of you—richer you, more hip and happening you. Hurry, hustle, be hungry for more, more, more! All of these opportunities are right at your fingertips, and you don't want to miss out. I have what it will take to deliver you from where you are to where you really want to be whether you realize it or not."

Identify specific areas where you see this playing out in your life.

Let's continue the story we were studying from yesterday by taking a closer look at Hezekiah's response and his need for a true deliverer.

Both King Hezekiah and his people found themselves in a deliverer dilemma. Would "the great king" of Assyria or the divine King of heaven truly be able to save them? As we continue to see through Scripture, repetition of words, phrases, and themes are important. The Hebrew word **natsal**, which is translated into English as "deliver," refers to being pulled out, saved, or removed.[46] This word is used thirteen times in Kings, and of those thirteen, twelve instances occur here in the story of Hezekiah (2 Kings 18–20).[47] It is clear that the people of God found themselves in desperate need of rescue, to be pulled out and saved from the circumstance they found themselves in.

Describe a circumstance in your life in which you longed for a rescuer.

Who or what did you turn to at that time for rescue or deliverance?

Read 2 Kings 19.

In verse 3, King Hezekiah clearly communicated how he had been attacked, and we find three ways his faith and trust could have been shattered. I think this is the same way we are attacked today.

Read verses 1-7 again and write how each of the following played out in this story:
• **Distress**

  He is threatend to be destroyed

• **Rebuke**

  He was told God wont provide

• **Disgrace**

  He denied the power of God

In the midst of these attacks, King Hezekiah modeled a response of what it looks like to put our trust wholly in the Lord.

> How did Hezekiah respond to the news (2 Kings 19:1)?
>
> *he tore his clothes, went to temple pray + sought Godly counsel.*

The first response is penance and pleading with the Lord. Hezekiah tore his clothes, covered himself with sackcloth, and entered the house of the Lord. His words resembled those of his forefather King David as David questioned those who would "defy the armies of the living God" (1 Sam. 17:26). Just as David placed his trust in the true Deliverer, Hezekiah followed in his footsteps. This connection is made even more clear with the usage of the word "mock," "defy," or "reproach" (depending on your translation).

> Look through 1 Samuel 17. How many times do you see that word used in the story of David and Goliath?
>
> *yes*

GOD'S PEOPLE HAVE NO NEED TO FEAR BECAUSE HE IS OUR DELIVERER.

"Mock" or "defy" is a key word used in the story of David and Goliath, describing the mockery of the Philistines against the Lord. This word is used in Kings only in the Hezekiah narrative (19:4,16,22,23).[48] These language connections continue to reinforce to us how Hezekiah took after David. They both returned to the Lord in the midst of their trouble.

> Go back to 2 Kings 19. How did God respond in verse 6?
>
> *Do not be afraid*
> *he tells him what he's going to do*
> *reassure him*

He responded the same way He always has throughout the course of human history. We have seen this response in Kings (1 Kings 17:13; 2 Kings 6:16), which is just a small sampling of the long history of God's command to be courageous in the midst of opposition because He is with us.

Look up the following verses and jot down the message from God in each one:

Genesis 15:1 *Do not be afraid, I am your shield*

Matthew 10:26 *"*

Matthew 14:27 *Take courage, it is I. Do not be afraid.*

Revelation 1:17 *Do not be afraid.*

Revelation 2:10 *Do not be afraid.*

God's people have no need to fear because He is our Deliverer. Even when it doesn't look exactly like we thought it would, God delivers us for our good and for His glory. God defends His people and defeats His enemies for His name's sake.

Write out 2 Kings 19:34.

I will defend this city + save it for my sake + the sake of David my servant

How exactly did God deliver His people? In 2 Kings 19:29-34 God gave King Hezekiah a sign. Let's pay close attention to the sequence of events that took place because it will be important for your next day of study: Hezekiah was in distress, he cried out to the Lord, the Lord responded, the Lord told Hezekiah how he would be delivered, and the Lord gave him a sign. A sign of God's deliverance was Israel's provision through the crops that were left and what "grows of itself" (v. 29). The word *grows* **(sāpiaḥ)** is the same one used in Leviticus 25:5,11, which refers to the seed left during the sabbatical year.[49]

Look up Leviticus 25:1-12. Though this crop was not to be sold or stored, what would it do for the people? (See vv. 6-7.)

> Why do you think God used the same language here in 2 Kings to refer to the sign of His deliverance?

The Israelites would have only gotten in part of the harvest before the attack of the Assyrians. This partial harvest would have been enough for them in the short term but would have been a source of concern for the following year. But God had an amazing plan. It is likely that the Assyrian army would have left around October, and it would have been too late for the Israelites to do the rest of the harvesting of the existing crop and replanting in preparation for the next year. However, God promised the seeds from the crops never harvested from that year would fall on the ground, producing a crop so bountiful that by the third year all would be recovered.[50] They would miraculously get more than if they had harvested and planted the field as originally planned before the attack.

The miracle was in their midst. It was already built into the way God designed seeds to work. Isn't that beautiful?

This is how God often delivers us. We can be tempted to look for the miraculous sign of deliverance, but God will often point us to what is already in front of us—evidence He has taken care of us in the past and of His pattern of faithfulness for our future.

> Look back at instances in your own life or in the lives of people you know. Are there "seeds" of provision? How has God proven Himself faithful to you personally in a recent circumstance?

> Close in prayer, thanking God for being the one true Deliverer, faithful to provide for and rescue us.

DEALING
with DOUBT

It's easy to believe God when everything goes according to our plans.

But what about when we assume we know what a good God would do and He doesn't do it our way? That's when things can start to get a bit complicated. It's the place where doubts are formed and disappointment grows. The place where we can be tempted to distance ourselves from God with a heart of distrust. Will God really be who He says He is?

> When in your life have you been tempted to distance yourself from God because you couldn't understand either His lack of activity or His doing something way different than what you expected?

For all the good King Hezekiah did, we need to remember he was still human and prone to doubt just like we all are.

Let's take a step back and just consider doubt. First, doubt is a common and honest human emotion. We have all experienced doubts about ourselves and even loved ones. We may not want to admit it, but we may have even experienced doubts about God and His goodness. On Day 2 we talked about King Hezekiah and fear. Today, we will unpack how King Hezekiah dealt with his doubt. Let's remember how strong King Hezekiah started his reign and rule, how he placed all his trust in the Lord. In 2 Kings 20 Hezekiah became sick. And suddenly, the king who was filled with trust battled doubt.

We can see this battle take place by comparing King Hezekiah's prayer in 2 Kings 19:15-19 and his prayer in 2 Kings 20:1-3.

How did Hezekiah address God in each prayer?

2 Kings 19:15-19	2 Kings 20:2-3
God of Israel you alone are God over all you made Heaven + Earth	Lord

How many sentences are in each prayer?

2 Kings 19:15-19	2 Kings 20:2-3
6	1

How would you describe the overall theme of each prayer?

2 Kings 19:15-19	2 Kings 20:2-3
Trusting Expecting	Desperate

Did you notice the subtle perspective shift of Hezekiah's prayers? His second prayer may seem more self-centered and less faith-centered than his earlier prayer. This is a very subtle but distinct shift of perspective that would create space for the development of doubt. It's not a bad or wrong thing for Hezekiah to cry out for healing. In fact God is our Father and He wants us to call out to Him (Ps. 105:1; 116:2). However, God also cares about the condition of our hearts and the motivations of our prayers.

Take a moment to examine your own prayer life. Is it more self-focused or God-focused?

Let's read 2 Kings 20:4-7. How did God respond to Hezekiah's prayer?

Not only did He promise healing, but God specified He would add fifteen years to Hezekiah's life and once again prove to be the Deliverer not only of Hezekiah's life but also of the city from the hand of the Assyrian king. If only the story stopped here. But it doesn't.

Let's read 2 Kings 20:8-11. What did Hezekiah ask for?

Why do you think he asked that?

The text doesn't tell us exactly why, but if it were me, there would be a lot of doubt swirling around in my head. Also, remember from Day 3, God gave a sign to Hezekiah before, so maybe getting a sign from God became an expectation for him. The reason we can see so much doubt is not simply because Hezekiah asked for a sign but because of how he worded what he wanted the sign to be!

Let's take a closer look at some details of Hezekiah's mind-set during the times of his two different prayers. You can refer back to your chart on the previous pages as we dig in more.

Remember, in King Hezekiah's prayer in chapter 19, he started with a declaration that God is the Creator of the heavens and earth. In chapter 20, Hezekiah asked God to make the shadow return ten steps.

What do these details from the text tell you about Hezekiah's mind-set?

Hezekiah's Tunnel

The mind-set here seems to be not one of trust but of distrust. He appeared to have a preconditioned mind-set of doubting what God promises. Instead of immediately being overwhelmed with gratitude at the faithfulness of the Lord, His immediate response to the news his illness would not kill him was a need of proof and reassurance.

Not only did Hezekiah want a sign, but he also controlled how the sign functioned. This was a chance for him to reply to Isaiah that he trusted God to have the shadow move any way. Instead, when asked by Isaiah about the direction that the shadow should move, Hezekiah chose to dictate the shadow to move in the most difficult direction.

It would be too easy for the shadow to lengthen but much more difficult for it to go backwards, and that is what Hezekiah wanted. It seems like Hezekiah wanted the more difficult sign to ease his doubts of God's faithfulness in His promise.

Often in Scripture the original language reveals symbolic overtones. Pay close attention to the phrase "return" or "go back ten steps" in verse 9. The Hebrew word for *return* is **šûb.**[51] It's used many times throughout the Bible in lots of different stories, but it reminds me of God's faithfulness.

How do you think the word *return* might speak to God's faithfulness? Think of stories in the Bible where a similar term might be used.

One of the stories I immediately thought of was the return of God's people from exile.

> Go ahead and finish reading 2 Kings 20. What did Isaiah prophesy would happen to the people of Judah?

In the Book of Isaiah, this same prophet prophesied that one day Judah would return to the promised land. According to Isaiah 44:28, Jerusalem would be rebuilt and the temple's foundation would be laid. God would be faithful to His promises.

This promise of a return from exile is a faithful promise for us today. God has promised the return of His Son, Jesus, who entered humanity as the King of kings to redeem and restore all that was lost by dying on the cross for our sins, raising to life after three days, and ascending into heaven. The people of Hezekiah's time waited on Jesus' first coming; we wait for Him to return and make all things new. Finally, the captives will return to the perfect presence of God and live under His perfect reign and rule.

We're about to shift to practical application of what we've been learning, but before we do, let's stop to give thanks for who God is. Today, may our prayers more closely resemble Hezekiah's in chapter 19.

> Take a moment to praise God for who He is, for His faithful love, and for the return of His Son one day.

So how do we reorient our mind-set on the faithfulness of God when we feel overwhelmed by doubt?

First, we can start with an intentional shift from having a self-centered mind-set to a faith-centered mind-set. Doubt in itself is not a bad thing, but when our doubts take us to a place of self-focus and not faith-focus, we lose sight of the mercy and magnitude of God.

This shift begins by returning to the truth of who God is. When we look at Hezekiah's prayer in 2 Kings 20, we see that he never even made an ask of God.

In fact, before that could even happen, God, through the prophet Isaiah, spoke to Hezekiah and said three faith-filling statements (v. 5).

> What three things did God tell Hezekiah through Isaiah in 2 Kings 20:5?

One of the ways we can battle the doubt in our lives is by preaching these truths about God to ourselves:

1. God hears us;

2. God sees us;

3. God will respond mercifully to us.

God extended great mercy and reassured Hezekiah by providing a sign. Sometimes God gives us signs that He is at work, but we don't need signs to confirm the truth of who God is and His work in our lives. The very essence of our faith is believing in what we cannot see.

> As we look not to the things that are seen but to the things that are unseen. For the things that are seen are transient, but the things that are unseen are eternal.
>
> 2 CORINTHIANS 4:18

WHEN OUR DOUBTS TAKE US TO A PLACE OF SELF-FOCUS AND NOT FAITH-FOCUS, WE LOSE SIGHT OF THE MERCY AND MAGNITUDE OF GOD.

The Lord will deal gently with our doubts, of that we can be sure. But let's make every effort to move toward a faith that is not tied to temporal things we can see but to the eternity God has set in our hearts (Eccl. 3:11)

FOR *the* MOST PART

Now, let's just get to the reason I feel so few Bible studies have been written around the ancient kings of Israel.

Just when I thought it was safe to throw a little party and tie Hezekiah's story up in a nice bow, I'm reminded of his utter humanity. I sit down and feel frustrated by even this king who is one of the most faithful we will study. It's complicated mixing the reality of humanity with the hope of divinity.

I feel like we really rallied around him at the beginning of this week. But as we've progressed we've seen even he faltered and failed at being the epic hero he could have been. Remember how I said in Day 1 that Hezekiah lived out his life (for the most part) from a place of dependence on God rather than depending on himself? This is where the "for the most part" really comes into play.

I have to remember the fact that God, as with David, gave this word about Hezekiah:

> He trusted in the LORD, the God of Israel, so that there was none like him among all the kings of Judah after him, nor among those who were before him.
>
> 2 KINGS 18:5

This statement gives me such great hope. Even though Hezekiah was not perfect in his trust and obedience, God still thought this way about him. God is not looking for perfection from us. After all, on this side of eternity perfection is unattainable. If it were, we would not have such a great need for Jesus.

What God is looking for is faithfulness and behavior patterns of returning to His Word and counsel when we come across situations that test our trust in Him.

> We find the end of Hezekiah's story in 2 Kings 20:12-21. Take a moment and reread this story.

In 2 Kings 20:12 we again meet the Babylonians, who will become the major enemy of the people of God. We can trace the drifting away of Hezekiah's trusting God to the acceptance of the gift from Babylon.

Some commentators view this gift as also being a subtle bribe presented to Hezekiah to encourage him to join them in revolting against Assyria.[52] Ultimately, Hezekiah sought to strengthen the kingdom's position and power through allegiance with Babylon rather than solely trusting in God. The Israelites knew God as the great I AM—a title that defined God as always being present and needing nothing. This is the God the Israelites were called to trust in. The great I AM is the only trustworthy One.

> Has there been a time where you realized you drifted away from trusting God? How did the drifting begin?

> Read 2 Kings 20:13 and Isaiah 39:2. These two accounts are almost identical with one subtle variation. What is the difference?

> You may remember Deuteronomy 17:17 from earlier in our study. Let's look at this verse again. How is King Hezekiah violating what God said?

> How can we know that King Hezekiah started to drift away from God through his pride in showing off "his" treasures?

When Hezekiah bragged/spoke of the treasures of the temple, he used what are translated into English as possessive pronouns, indicating *he* was the owner of the building and the temple.

> What could that indicate about Hezekiah's heart?

> Look again at verse 13 and count how many times Hezekiah is referred to as the owner of a place or item. Jot down the items that are said to be "his" as well.

Let's take a moment and really unpack this. Hezekiah decided to take these guests (who were strangers and possible future enemies) on a personal tour of his house to see all "his" treasuries. By bragging about his wealth, he made his future enemy aware of just how much treasure was in the temple, the palace, and the whole realm. He not only exposed himself but his whole country.

> What do you think was Hezekiah's motivation in doing this?

Before we go too far into Hezekiah's pride here, it may be good to do a little self-examination. He exposed his possessions most likely in an attempt to show his value or worth. Looking at this motivation is key. He wasn't just being hospitable to his guests. He was elevating his worth by taking credit for his wealth.

It may be hard for us to be honest enough with ourselves to admit we sometimes do this very thing. Have you ever attached your worth and value to the wrong things? Instead of letting what you've been entrusted with elevate the faithfulness of God, maybe you're tempted to let it elevate "your" significance.

> Write your thoughts here. Remember, this isn't meant to be an accusation but rather a revelation to help us see where this might be happening in our lives.

The use of the possessive pronouns that underlie this passage shows us how connected Hezekiah was to "his" possessions.

> How could we better pay attention to the possessive pronouns we use in our own lives?

This is a direct contradiction to what God intended for the kings of His people.

Many times, we may not see how this plays out in our own lives, the gradual reliance on things other than the One who is trustworthy. Hezekiah built up literal treasuries and relied on them to keep him safe.

> Ask the Lord to help you see what pattern of distrust could potentially be forming in your life. Write any thoughts that come to mind below.

Now I'm not a motorcycle expert by any stretch of the imagination. Nor have I ever operated a motorcycle. But I came across some interesting research about something called countersteering. When you're riding a motorcycle and making a turn, you lean in the opposite direction to provide some balance to your turn. If you lean in the same direction as your turn, you will topple the bike over. This countersteering approach doesn't just apply to riding a bike.

When you start to drift away from trusting God, you can counterbalance this turn by intentionally leaning back toward God. Think of how differently we might read the end of Hezekiah's story if, instead of using the kingdom's treasure to elevate himself, he elevated the presence and provision of God. There is power in leaning into the presence and provision of God.

> How can you elevate the presence and provision of God in your life? Jot down a few ideas and try implementing one of them this week.

Another act of distrust by Hezekiah can be found in 2 Kings 20:19, when he called the future prophecy from Isaiah "good." As one commentator put it, "This is a clear public attitude of resignation to the word of God on the part of the king."[53]

How did Hezekiah's response to Isaiah's words demonstrate a lack of trust?

He showed that he loved himself more than the kingdom of God.

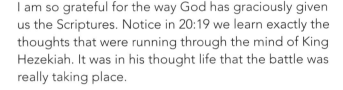

THE BATTLE IS EITHER WON OR LOST BASED ON THE DECISIONS THAT FLOW FROM OUR MINDS.

I am so grateful for the way God has graciously given us the Scriptures. Notice in 20:19 we learn exactly the thoughts that were running through the mind of King Hezekiah. It was in his thought life that the battle was really taking place.

Friends, it's in *our* thought life that the battle is really taking place. The battle is either won or lost based on the decisions that flow from our minds. This is why it's so important to take our thoughts captive and place them under the authority of Jesus.

Consider 2 Corinthians 10:1-6. What does this passage mean when it says our battle isn't against flesh?

How would remembering that have helped Hezekiah in his reign?

How do we take thoughts captive?

The only way for the battle to truly be won is when it's fought with the mind of Christ (1 Cor. 2:16; 1 Pet. 1:13). Here is the good news: to have the mind of Christ is to receive what we have been freely given by God the Father through the Holy Spirit. So let's always pause to call on the Spirit to help us think with the mind of Christ.

It's at this point in the life of Hezekiah where we drop our heads in despair and say, "Not again!" However, let's not miss the journey that Hezekiah found himself on. It is not just Hezekiah's journey; it's our journey as well.

1. Hezekiah left a moment of miraculous healing and was almost immediately faced with a test of trust he probably didn't even realize was taking place;

2. Hezekiah received a gift within the context of his great need;

3. The need to prove himself and his worth drove him away from the only One worthy of our trust;

4. Hezekiah settled for a short-lived best, not the long-term best for his people.

Which of these aspects of Hezekiah's story most speaks to you today? The details aren't the same, but which one do you most closely identify with?

How is God asking you to trust Him today?

Learning deeper trust in God doesn't often happen in straight lines of obedience. It's when we cycle through trials, tripping and sometimes falling, that we realize our desperate need for Him. Knowing our need for Him leads us to putting our trust in Him.

THE IMPACT OF IDOLATRY ON THE PEOPLE OF GOD

The epitome of the creation story is when God created man and breathed life into him (Gen. 2:7). God did something different with humankind that separated us from all other created things. God created humankind (Adam and Eve) in His likeness and image (Gen. 1:27). Therefore, humanity bears the very dignity of God because we were created to resemble God.

In Genesis 3 we learn that Adam and Eve fell prey to the temptation of the serpent. The nature of the temptation presented by the serpent is what we call idolatry today. Idolatry is trusting, serving, or giving worship to something that is not God.

Adam and Eve were tempted to believe that God was withholding something good from them. As a result, they idolized the thought of being like God. They ate the fruit God told them not to eat because it could give them wisdom that would make them more like God. The tremendous irony is that they were already like God—remember, they were made in the image of God. God had already entrusted to them as much knowledge as the human heart and mind could manage. The knowledge of evil was a heavy weight. God wasn't withholding from them; He was protecting them.

The impact of idolatry has plagued humanity ever since.

If we trace the biblical story, we will find the subtle yet specific theme of idolatry negatively impacting the people of God. But what is this impact? Every time we find ourselves being drawn to worship something and give it more affection than we give to God, we begin to reflect that idolatrous object, which will ultimately lead us to ruin. This is exactly what we find throughout the Old Testament. Isaiah 6 is an example where we see both realities at play. If we pay close attention to the description in Isaiah 6:8-9 we find characteristics of a people who resemble the very nature of the idols they worship. Remember, the idols have no life, strength, power, or capacity to create or act. In other words, they are unable to hear, see, understand, or provide us with anything. They are utterly worthless. Now notice Isaiah's description of the people:

1. They keep hearing but don't understand.
2. They see but don't perceive.

The prophet Habakkuk developed this thought further in Habakkuk 2:18-19, when he argued the worthlessness of an idol when a human shapes and creates it. How can the creator trust his own creation for his own salvation? How can someone look at a created wooden object and ask it to arise and become alive? When we do these things, we begin to reflect these idols. Theologian G. K. Beale wrote, "We resemble what we revere, either for our ruin or restoration."[54]

So, what is the object of your reverence? In Isaiah 6:1-6 we find that Isaiah's object of reverence was God. Therefore, God purified, anointed, and restored him so he could do the work of the Lord.

Today, when we submit ourselves to Christ and make Him the object of our affection and reverence, the Spirit of God brings about our restoration. Our restoration includes both right relationship with God and returning to the original design of humanity to reflect the likeness and image of God. The perfect imprint of God came in Christ Jesus. So our journey toward God is a journey toward becoming more Christlike.

VIDEO SESSION 5: HEZEKIAH

WATCH VIDEO SESSION 5 AND RECORD YOUR NOTES BELOW.

_____

_____

_____

_____

_____

_____

_____

_____

_____

_____

_____

_____

_____

_____

_____

_____

_____

_____

_____

_____

_____

_____

_____

_____

_____

group guide

VIDEO GROUP DISCUSSION QUESTIONS

After watching the video, discuss the following questions in your group.

- What is the significance of Hezekiah's Tunnel and the Pool of Siloam? How are they both important physically and spiritually?

- What are some truths you learned about Hezekiah from the passages?

- How are we often like Hezekiah—cycling from faithful to unfaithful and back again?

- How have you seen God's faithfulness in your life?

- What are some ways you are demonstrating that you are trustworthy with what God has given to you?

To access the video teaching sessions, use the instructions in the back of your Bible study book.

159

Josiah

AND THOSE WHO KNOW YOUR NAME PUT THEIR TRUST IN YOU, FOR YOU, O LORD, HAVE NOT FORSAKEN THOSE WHO SEEK YOU.

PSALM 9:10

#TRUSTWORTHYSTUDY

Connecting the Kings

Remember, the Northern Kingdom of Israel was in exile during this time because the Assyrians had conquered them (2 Kings 17:6). Only two kings reigned in Judah between Hezekiah and Josiah, whom we'll study this week. One was Manasseh, Hezekiah's son. Manasseh became king at age twelve and immediately set about rebuilding the high places his father had destroyed. You can read a lot of his story in 2 Kings 21, but an interesting fact about his life is found in 2 Chronicles 33. After being captured, Manasseh repented of his wrongdoing, and verse 13 says, "Then Manasseh knew that the LORD is God." From that passage, we see him trying to undo the evil he had done

NORTHERN KINGDOM

ISRAEL—CAPITAL: SAMARIA

FALL OF SAMARIA
722 BC

As a result, some of the Northern Kingdom went into exile while some of the people fled and went to find help and shelter in the Southern Kingdom of Judah.

740 BC   720 BC   700 BC   680 BC

MANASSEH
696-642 BC

SOUTHERN KINGDOM

JUDAH—CAPITAL: JERUSALEM

To study more about the kings, please see the Guide to 1 & 2 Kings on page 207.

*Please note: The dates listed are the approximate years each king reigned. Due to co-regency and other variables, these dates may vary by source.

during his reign. I love the story of grace there—God can redeem anyone.

Manasseh's son Amon reigned after him and once again did evil in the sight of the Lord. We also read about him in 2 Kings 21. Second Chronicles 33 notes that Amon did not repent like his father, but instead

"incurred guilt more and more" (v. 23). Into this lineage, Josiah was born.

After Josiah, the rest of 2 Kings details the reigns of four more kings before Judah fell into Babylonian captivity around 586 BC.[55]

ISRAEL

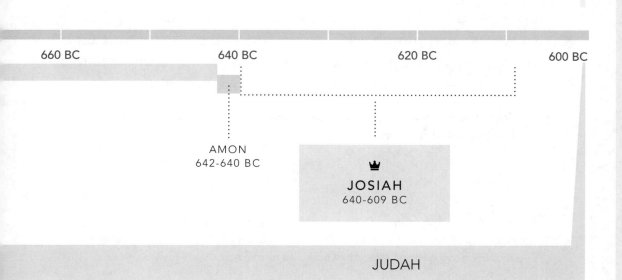

660 BC   640 BC   620 BC   600 BC

AMON
642-640 BC

♛

JOSIAH
640-609 BC

JUDAH

the BEGINNING of the STORY

In other weeks, we've let the life lesson of the king emerge as we studied. But this week, I want to hint at the lesson to provide a little context right up front. Josiah was one of the few good kings. The biggest lesson I've learned from him is setting a pattern in life to remember and revisit the faithfulness of God. When current events don't feel like they are in keeping with a God who is in control and completely able to be trusted, we have to have strong reminders. These patterns of remembering drive the stake of trusting God so deeply into our belief systems that His faithfulness is automatically factored in to whatever we are processing.

> Take a few minutes and write down times you remember when God has been faithful to you.

The past three years of my life have been the hardest I've ever walked through. Some people have referred to this season of my life as one where I've experienced a lot of attack because I'm in ministry.

To some extent this may be true.

But I think of it a little differently based on seeing everything in my life from the vantage point of God's faithfulness. I honestly believe that God saw all I would be facing in my life in this season and intentionally put me in ministry years ago. Being in ministry has given me an intense intentionality to study God's Word in ways I probably wouldn't have otherwise. And being in ministry has placed deadlines on writing and processing my studies with a deep sense of responsibility that may not have been there otherwise.

I'm not saying I wouldn't have studied and written if I wasn't in ministry. But what I am saying is deadlines and expectations of my calling forced me to do it all the more urgently and completely than ever before. I think it was God's mercy for my typical procrastinating personality to place me in ministry and to prepare me in those days for what He knew I would face in these days.

But you don't have to be placed in ministry to develop this kind of urgency. We just have to realize how crucial it is to get into God's Word and have His Word get into us right now. It's no mistake you are doing this study right now. And I think it's God's mercy to prepare you today for what you'll need one day. It may be something complicated coming your way. Or something hard. Or even a blessing that He needs to prepare you for. Whatever it is, God's Word is your lifeline. When instruction from God's Word is what we heed, we are more able to discern His direction for what we need.

Being saturated in God's Word today prepares us to walk securely in His faithfulness tomorrow.

> What are some ways you can be saturated in God's Word in your everyday? Try thinking outside the box of simply reading the Bible (though that is important too).

WHEN INSTRUCTION FROM GOD'S WORD IS WHAT WE HEED, WE ARE MORE ABLE TO DISCERN HIS DIRECTION FOR WHAT WE NEED.

We must remember that keeping God's Word at the forefront is just as crucial for the tasks ahead of us as it was for the kings we've been studying and the tasks they encountered in their reigns. We see things around us that aren't right. We recognize things that need to be changed. We identify what isn't in keeping with God's Word. So, we have a choice to make a difference or not.

The ancient kings had to decide if they would be complacent in culture or obedient to God. We have the same choice to make.

Let's review the kings we've studied so far. Match each king to his description.

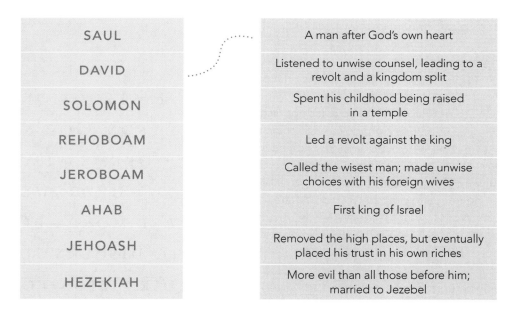

SAUL	A man after God's own heart
DAVID	Listened to unwise counsel, leading to a revolt and a kingdom split
SOLOMON	Spent his childhood being raised in a temple
REHOBOAM	Led a revolt against the king
JEROBOAM	Called the wisest man; made unwise choices with his foreign wives
AHAB	First king of Israel
JEHOASH	Removed the high places, but eventually placed his trust in his own riches
HEZEKIAH	More evil than all those before him; married to Jezebel

King Josiah, one of the final kings of Judah, was one who chose wisely. Under King Josiah's rule and reign, Judah experienced its last glimpse of stability and thriving due to his faithfulness and doing what was right in the sight of the Lord. Like Jehoash, Josiah started his reign very young. Jehoash was seven years old and Josiah was only eight.

Read 2 Kings 21:10-18. Manassah was Josiah's grandfather. According to these verses, what kind of king was Manasseh?

He was sinful, led his people to sin, + killed so many ppl.

Flip over to 2 Chronicles 33:10-20. What does this passage bring to light about the end of Manasseh's life?

He repented + God restored his kingdom

What is discouraging about Manasseh's story? What is encouraging?

He took so long to see god + needed to be shackled.

Now read 2 Kings 21:19-24 and note what Josiah's father was like as king. What happened for Josiah to become king at such a young age?

Amon's officials assassinated him.

Josiah's lineage is complicated and doesn't seem to point in the direction of him becoming a king who honored God. Maybe you look at your lineage and see more hardship than hope. But Josiah made different choices than his father and grandfather and so can we. One beautiful reality in Josiah's family is the name of his mother—Jedidah, which is the feminine form of Jedidiah (2 Kings 22:1). Do you remember the last time we studied that name?

What do you remember about the name Jedidiah?

Beloved

This name means "beloved" and was the name given to David and Bathsheba's second son, whom we more popularly call Solomon. Jedidah and Jedidiah are both woven into stories where redemption can be found.

Names carried a lot of weight in ancient times. How does this name being included in both of these stories speak to you personally?

My biological father completely rejected my sister and me when we were very young. His absence broke our hearts and left us with deep wounds from being abandoned. However, I remember finding a book of his poetry once that fascinated me and stirred inside of me a curiosity about the power of stringing words together. Though I don't have a rich legacy passed from my father to me, I know my love for writing came from him. It's a redemptive aspect in my life story that makes me smile: God was so faithful even if it didn't play out with my father returning and reconciling with me and my sister. A good part of him became a good part of me.

What is a redemptive aspect of your lineage that highlights the faithfulness of God working in the midst of even unfaithful people?

Record 2 Kings 22:2 here.

He did what was right in the eyes of the Lord

Let's not forget how important the lineage of David was. Yes, Josiah came from David's line! And as this week unfolds it will become even more important to remember that our ultimate King, Jesus, will also come from this family's line.

Now read 2 Chronicles 34:1-7. What did Josiah do that so many kings before him failed to do? (Note: we read about Hezekiah doing the same thing last week.)

Thinking back to our very first week, why was this so important?

Josiah brought reform to the people of God in a significant way. That might sound like a far-off need for "other" people, but we are desperately in need of reform in our lives today. We need to recognize the patterns of false worship and actively renounce the objects of our affections that are competing for our attention. As we study King Josiah we will identify some of the most important spiritual practices for us to exercise and commit to. First, let's consider the patterns of the good kings we have studied.

1. Notice that most of the "good" kings followed a king who was "evil." Their immediate predecessors were said to have done "evil in the sight of the LORD" (1 Kings 15:26). Each of the evil kings worshiped false Canaanite gods and therefore led the people of God into idolatry and false worship. All of the kings after Saul stepped into a landscape of leadership and kingship that was truly broken. The work in front of them was not easy; they were not set up for success. In fact, they were perfectly set up to continue in the paths of wickedness and evil. What the good kings embarked on to turn the attention and affection of the people of Israel back to their God was a monumental task.

2. Each of these good kings battled a common enemy. You may be racking your brain to remember who those enemies were. The Egyptians, the Assyrians, the Babylonians? Yes, but no. They were enemies, but the greater enemy was idolatry, and the common false gods that kept showing up to tempt and torment the people of God were from those countries.

3. In the Southern Kingdom (Judah), reform involved temple repair, reorganization, and rebuilding temple life and culture.

4. Finally, none of the reforms concludes ideally.

Remember, these are not patterns and situations isolated to the kings.

How do you see similar patterns in today's culture that threaten to influence the church?

How do you see similar patterns in your life?

We find ourselves in these same situations. When was the last time you entered a work or home environment where things were an absolute mess? You have the opportunity to leave it that way or to start implementing positive change.

> What are the struggles you've seen present themselves over and over again in your life? What keeps showing up, maybe in new and unique ways but the essence is always the same? It may be doubt in provision and finances, concern over family, or a struggle with a certain sin.

Our response to these struggles, just like the good kings, should be a repair of the temple. The kings repaired a physical temple; however, today we know that we are the actual temple of the Lord. Remember, we learned that 1 Corinthians 6:19 says:

> Or do you not know that your body is a temple of the Holy Spirit within you, whom you have from God? You are not your own.

So there is repair and rebuilding that needs to take place in our lives as a result of sin or negative patterns that play out in our hearts, minds, and souls. It's time for a renovation.

> We are now the temple. What does renovation of our temples look like today? What is the first step?

The major difference between the good kings and our stories is the ending. The ending of each reign was overwhelmingly not ideal as each king's time on earth came to an end. We know the end to our story in Christ Jesus. Because of the finished work of Christ on the cross we can be assured of our redemption and restoration of right relationship with the true King of kings!

FINDING *the* BOOK *of the* LAW

As we read through the story of Josiah it would be very helpful to also consider the additional details included in the Book of 2 Chronicles like we did in Day 1. The author of this book is often referred to as the "Chronicler." This is simply a title that defines what was done—he chronicled the events that took place during the reigns of the kings.

> Look back at 2 Kings 22:1-2 and 2 Chronicles 34:1-3. Compare the two passages—what is similar and what is unique?

Josiah "began to seek the God of David his father" (2 Chron. 34:3a) at an early age—notice the detail that this was done "while he was yet a boy." Each of our stories is different. Some of us have grown up surrounded with church, the Bible, and Christians. For some of us, God graciously rescued and saved us later in life. Regardless of the when, how incredible is it that He saved us!

> GOD ISN'T TRYING TO HIDE FROM US. HE IS WAITING TO BE SEEN BY US.

Take a moment to go back to that time and location and reflect on what you did after your first encounter with the Lord. Jot down a few memories of that moment. If you were very young, write down some of your earliest memories of hearing about God.

I love what theologian and scholar G. K. Beale says, and I think it's worth quoting again: "We resemble what we revere, either for our ruin or restoration."[56] King Josiah sought after the Lord and therefore his actions reflected the One whom he revered. The result? The restoration of the people of God for a season under the rule and reign of this righteous and upright king.

What does it mean to *revere*? Look up the word in a dictionary or online if you need to and then write the definition in your own words.

How did Josiah's seeking God demonstrate his reverence of Him?

King Josiah's seeking resulted in repairing the temple of the Lord. In that process an incredible discovery was made.

Let's read 2 Kings 22:8-12. What was discovered?

In these verses, we meet Hilkiah the high priest. The high priest had a very important role in temple life and in relationship between God and His people. Once a year, the high priest would enter into the holy of holies (the innermost part of the temple) to make a sacrifice and commune with the Lord on behalf of the people. The high priest was responsible to know and make known the Word of the Lord called the "Book of the Law." The Book of the Law first appears in

Deuteronomy in reference to the teachings that were given to Israel by Moses before entering Canaan (Deut. 28:61).

Before we get too far into this passage, let's remember what we've read previously in Deuteronomy so we can take into account the importance of how Josiah responded to the Book of the Law.

> Read Deuteronomy 17:18-20. Why was the Book of the Law important for the kings?

GOD'S WORD MUST LEAD MY THOUGHTS, NOT THE OTHER WAY AROUND.

> What should be the response to the Book of the Law?

Someone posed a poignant question to me the other day: Do I read God's Word to prove the thoughts I bring to the text? Or do I let the text shape my thoughts I will then apply to my life? (See box below for further information on this.)

God's Word must lead my thoughts, not the other way around.

My response to His Word is very telling of how I view His Word. If it's an ancient book with some good principles, I will read it and take from it what I want. But if I truly believe the Bible is the living Word of the one true and holy God, I don't just read it; I let it read me. It will breathe fresh life into me, rearrange my wrong thinking, redirect my wayward heart tendencies, and cause me to become more and more humble with each interaction. It's not just a book. Though it chronicles events past tense, the Bible is God's Word speaking to us in present tense.

> *Exegesis: A word-by-word study of Scripture that brings themes and teachings out of the text. The text both informs and confirms theories around the topic at hand. This is also called "line-by-line teaching."*
>
> *Eisegesis: Starting with your theories on a topic and then looking for Bible verses to support your opinions. This is also called "cherry picking verses." You risk taking verses out of their intended context and applying them incorrectly.*

How do you allow the Bible to reveal possible hidden motives or places where your heart needs to be reoriented to the truth?

For example, if I'm feeling resistant to forgiving someone, do I let verses about forgiveness challenge my thinking and give space in my perspective to be convicted? Or do I look for ways to justify my thinking and sidestep opportunities to be convicted?

As we read through 2 Kings 22:8-12 it's really interesting to note how Hilkiah and Shaphan both viewed the Book of the Law. Notice how Hilkiah referred to it by its proper name. However, when Shaphan delivered the message to King Josiah, he simply said that he had been given "a book" (2 Kings 22:10). Clearly, the importance and reverence of this book was lost on Shaphan; however, the response of King Josiah helps us to see the importance of the words of the Lord.

Look at 2 Kings 22:11 again. What was Josiah's immediate response to hearing the Book of the Law read aloud?

Why do you think he responded in that way?

It's so interesting to compare how differently a good king and an evil king responded to the word of the Lord. Sadly, as we continue reading the story of the ancient kings, we will find that Josiah's son Jehoiakim responded to the written word of the Lord from the prophet Jeremiah by tearing the word of God and burning it in the flames (Jer. 36:23).

This begs us to ask the question: How will we respond to the Word when it is presented to us? Will we be torn in our hearts and drawn to repentance and worship? This is the right response to God's Word.

Josiah not only responded emotionally to the reading of the Word but reacted intentionally. It seems that, almost exclusively up to this point in 1 and 2 Kings, the kings of Israel and Judah only inquired of the Lord during times of personal illness, threatening enemies, or impending war (1 Kings 14:5; 22:5,7,8; 2 Kings 1:2,3,6,16; 3:11; 8:8). But with Josiah we see for the first time a king inquiring of the Lord primarily for imminent threat of his personal sin—not for an external enemy from another country but for the internal enemy of his own propensity for sin.

Let's pay close attention to what King Josiah did in terms of his reaction to hearing God's Word.

> Look at 2 Kings 22:12-13. How else did he respond to hearing God's Word?

> What did Josiah say his ancestors did in response to the Book of the Law? Why was this such a bad thing?

Humility in the reading of God's Word—what an important biblical concept that is so easily overlooked and discounted in our culture!

Josiah then instructed Hilkiah to go and "inquire of the LORD" (v. 13). Verse 14 lets us know Josiah's men intentionally went to a prophetess named Huldah. She is the only prophetess in all of Kings. It seems that her marriage to the "keeper of the wardrobe" (2 Kings 22:14) connected her to the royal court and placed her in close proximity to the palace because of her residence in Jerusalem.[57] What an amazingly simple but specific truth that helps us see God can and does use anyone—man or woman, Jew or Gentile, any social class. We are all made in the image of God and therefore hold dignity as bearers of God's divine image. We only hear from Huldah here, and her message was not easy for Josiah to hear. But she delivered it directly from the Lord.

This makes me pause and feel challenged. This woman had an unusual opportunity to interact with the most powerful people in her kingdom. It was crucial she deliver the warning from God exactly as she did. She didn't seem to struggle with people-pleasing and watering down the hard words she was given by God to deliver. Nor did she add her own commentary, opinions, or judgment into the mix. She was just faithful with a hard assignment.

Read Huldah's message (2 Kings 22:15-20) and write below how we can know she delivered only God's words and not her own.

Huldah was in a long tradition of people being assigned by God to be His spokesman or spokeswoman. The actual Hebrew words for *prophet* and *prophetess* mean "one who is called to speak."[58] Think of it as the prophets being a loudspeaker. The loudspeaker by itself has no voice or message. It needs a message spoken into it in order to be effective.

God spoke through Huldah to amplify His message to the people.

Before we take this section of Scripture as permission to start speaking on behalf of God or say, "This is what the Lord told me to tell you ..." remember how serious it was for a prophet or prophetess to wrongly deliver the words of the Lord. They would be put to death (Deut. 18:20). Prophets did not take their assignment lightly or without great consideration.

Today, we have the Holy Spirit to communicate and confirm God's will directly to our hearts. His messages are always in line with the Bible, God's Holy Word. This isn't to say we can't hold people accountable, but we must make sure our motives and words are being guided by God's Word.

Though Huldah's prophetic words were hard to hear, she also communicated God's grace toward Josiah.

Record below the two observations revealed about Josiah's heart in 2 Kings 22:19.

How does this challenge you personally? Are there areas where you need to be more responsive to God's Word and/or demonstrate humility in receiving God's Word?

The idea of being humbled comes from the Hebrew word כנע **(kāna)**, which is repeated in 2 Chronicles through many of the kings' lives and, therefore, an important thematic word. Some of the kings are humble and some are not. (See 2 Chron. 32:26; 33:12,19,23.)[59] We've seen Josiah's humble response to the reading of God's Word—to inquire of the Lord's prophetess. And we've seen Josiah's humble reaction to the challenging words Huldah delivered from the Lord. Humility in his response protected him from a sinful reaction.

How would you define *humility*? Do you see it as a sign of strength or weakness?

What do the following passages tell us humility looks like for the people of God?

2 Chronicles 7:14

Proverbs 22:4

Matthew 23:8-12

Romans 12:3,16

Philppians 2:3-4

Who is the most humble person you know? Why do you think that about this individual?

Back to Josiah and the Book of the Law. Here's the progression of events so far:

Josiah heard the reading of God's Word. He inquired of the Lord through the prophetess, Huldah. He received her strong correction and encouragement.

The Torah Scroll found in Jerusalem

Then he acted by reading the Book of the Law to the people and enacted strong reform.

He heard, he inquired, he received the message, and then he responded both personally and publicly.

Does this progression speak to the way we react when we hear God's Word taught today? Write out your thoughts below.

We hear God's Word.

Then we are to inquire of the Lord.

We have to personally receive the message.

And then we have to respond both personally and publicly to God's message.

End today by writing out a prayer, asking God to help you apply this pattern to your life this week.

JOSIAH'S *reform*

If I'm completely honest about the struggle I sometimes have with trusting God, it has very little, if anything, to do with God at all.

My trust issues stem from other relationships where the trust has been so severely broken that it left deep wounds inside me where trusting feels improbable at best and unsafe at worst. My biological father left us when he should have protected us. A college boyfriend I thought I was going to marry suddenly broke up with me to date someone new. A friend I thought would be a forever relationship was surprisingly unwilling to work through a disagreement. And there were other situations that left me with lingering hurt and heartbreak to work through as well.

While my brain knows that these are imperfect relationships full of human frailties that God doesn't have, I still have residual pain and hesitancies with trust that affect my relationship with God. It's not that I don't want to fully trust God. It's just that trusting is complicated for me. It's not complicated for God. But the simplicity of trusting God has been tainted by the complexities of trusting people.

How has trust become complicated for you?

The difference is that while relationships—even relationships with promises—can be broken with people and by people, the covenant promises God makes with us cannot and will not be broken by Him. This is what makes God's covenant commitment to us so special and unique.

WHILE OUR
TRUST CAN BE
BROKEN IN
RELATIONSHIP
WITH PEOPLE,
OUR TRUST
CAN BE
RESTORED IN
RELATIONSHIP
WITH GOD.

While our trust can be broken in relationship with people, our trust can be restored in relationship with God.

Read that last sentence again. How would you describe the difference between trust in relationships with people and trust in relationship with God?

This is why it is important for us to take time to really understand what the Bible has to say about God and His covenant with His people. Otherwise, we may try to process our understanding of the faithfulness of God through a tainted lens colored by the unfaithfulness of broken people. But if we learn to start processing life with a complete trust in the faithfulness of God, it can give us the solid ground we crave and grace for people who have hurt us.

What is the first thing that comes to your mind when you hear the word *covenant*?

Most likely, covenant isn't a word you walk around saying very often. However, it is a deeply rich and important concept in the Bible. C. C. Newman says, "'Covenant' implies relationship, promise and expectation. Within the biblical tradition the covenant points to the unique relationship Yahweh established with the world through Israel, Yahweh's immutable and sacred pledge of faithfulness to this special relationship and Yahweh's legitimate expectation for his people to respond appropriately (i.e. to live as covenant people)."[60]

When you think of covenants in the Bible, are there any that come to mind? (If you can't think of any, don't worry! We'll look at a few specific ones in a minute.)

Throughout the Bible, we see covenant after covenant made between God and humanity. A covenant ties together relationship, promise, and a binding agreement. In the covenants we see in Scripture, God is the initiator and the One who sees the promise to completion.

In today's study we will see how important the covenant was to King Josiah and how he reestablished the Israelites' responsibility to return to the Lord in both thought and deed because of their covenant relationship. But before we get into Josiah's story let's look at the idea of the covenant further.

The first time we see promise of the covenant is all the way back in Genesis 3:15. This is God's response to Adam and Eve's sin, also called the fall. This verse is known as the *Protevangelium*, a Latin term meaning "first gospel."[61] It specifically refers to the first promise of God with humankind. The promise assured that even though, through Adam and Eve, we brought death upon ourselves through sin, God would conquer sin and overcome death, bringing life through the divine Son of God—King Jesus, the promised Messiah.

Let's consider a few other covenants from Scripture. Some of these passages are a bit longer, so just look through the verses if you don't have time to read them word for word. Beside each passage, jot down a few things each covenant teaches you about God and His character.

Genesis 15

Exodus 19:1-9

2 Samuel 7:1-17

Jeremiah 31:31-34; Matthew 26:26-29

Covenant becomes an important theme in the story of Josiah. He read the Book of the Law to all the people. But notice what the book is called in 2 Kings 23:1-3 —"the Book of the Covenant." The fact that the Book of the Law is referred to as the Book of the Covenant reminded the king and his people that they were first and foremost involved in a covenant relationship with the Lord. To be in a covenant with the Lord was to be connected to the divine King.

When King Josiah read the Book of the Law he was reminded of the covenant promises and faithfulness of God. This had such a significant impact on him that he stood up amongst all of his people and called them to return to the Lord in all their ways.

> **This monumental moment is captured in 2 Kings 23:3. Take a moment to read this verse and write out your observations.**

I think it's interesting that, often in our journey through the stories of the kings, the act of restoring and reestablishing covenant is done primarily through God graciously calling His people to repentance. Again, we've seen God calling His people to repentance most often as a result of some kind of hardship (famine, war, political threats). However, uniquely in the story of Josiah the impulse and initiation of covenant renewal was brought about by King Josiah hearing and responding to the words of God.

When we read and hear the words of God in humility, what happens next? Notice for Josiah that humility didn't equate to passivity. Rather, it propelled him into action to do the right thing. His aggressive determination was to "perform" all the words of the covenant (2 Kings 23:3).

Sometimes when I see this word *perform*, I think of a performance in connection to a show. That's not the meaning of the word here. Here, it's used to indicate Josiah's full obedience.

We see his obedience clearly through his actions, and we can also see it in the actions of the people who joined in on this covenant renewal. In some of your Bible translations you may see in 2 Kings 23:3b that all the people "joined" or "pledged" themselves. The original Hebrew here is עָמַד **(āmaḏ)** and can literally be translated as "taking a stand."[62] The people would not simply agree and follow along. No. They would act and stand up, determined to follow Josiah and the words of the Law.

How does "taking a stand" speak to the resoluteness of the people to follow God's Law?

Remember, this isn't taking a stand against other people. This is taking a stand for God's Word in your own personal faith. Using 2 Kings 23:3b and humility as your guide, write your faith declaration here.

The most visible expression of returning to the Lord was for the people of God to return to the practice of the Passover.

Take a moment and read 2 Kings 23:21-23.

Did you catch that? The Passover, one of the most important celebrations for the Israelites, was forgotten from memory and lost for years. Since the days of the judges, this feast commanded by God was not practiced amongst the people of the Lord! The Levitical priesthood was in shambles and the temple was in total disrepair up until this point, when King Josiah rectified these issues.

God instituted the Passover in Exodus 12 as He rescued the Israelites from Egypt. God told the Israelites to put the blood of a lamb on their doorways to signify they were His and should be spared from the tenth and final plague on

PRAISE GOD FOR BEING THE COVENANT MAKER AND THE COVENANT KEEPER.

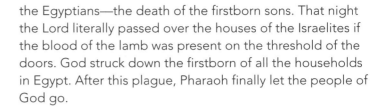

the Egyptians—the death of the firstborn sons. That night the Lord literally passed over the houses of the Israelites if the blood of the lamb was present on the threshold of the doors. God struck down the firstborn of all the households in Egypt. After this plague, Pharaoh finally let the people of God go.

God instituted Passover as a yearly celebration for the people to remember His faithful work in their past, serving as a reminder to continue in their walk toward the Lord.

Read 2 Kings 23:24-25. What did Josiah do next? How was this different from the kings before him?

Turn to Exodus 20:1-6. How did Josiah's actions in 2 Kings 23:24-25 demonstrate obedience to these laws?

We'll talk more about the importance of covenant, Josiah, and his obedience to the Lord tomorrow. This day of study had a lot of digging into the Word. I'm so thankful you did that with me. Let's close today in a way similar to Josiah after he read the Book of the Law. Let's receive what we have learned and put it into practice.

Give thanks for the holy and true Word of God. Praise God for being the covenant Maker and the covenant Keeper, for giving us a new covenant and writing grace on our hearts. Ask Him to help you as you put into practice what you're learning from Him.

ELIMINATING
distractions

What we see as we continue to study Josiah is a predetermined inclination toward trusting God. In other words, Josiah was so resolved ahead of time to trust God that it overrode other human tendencies.

This wasn't because trusting God was more woven into his personality or motivational makeup as a human, but rather because trusting God and following Him wholeheartedly was an established pattern in his daily routines.

I'm personally challenged by this. Sometimes when I read about the great faith of people in the Bible it's easy for me to wrongly assume God simply made them full of faith. Therefore, it's easier for me to say, "Good for them, but that's probably not possible for someone like me."

> Have you ever given yourself an out like that for becoming a person who truly and completely trusts God?

As we have already studied, Josiah was committed to the Lord. He sought after the Lord, and it seems he did his best to ensure that the will of the Lord based on the Word of the Lord was his guide. It's interesting to note that Josiah had social pressures in his day that could have pulled him away from completely trusting God, in the same way we do. One of those social pressures—for all the kings, including Josiah—was the widely accepted practice of going to the high places. Even though God was clear this was not acceptable for His people, the practice continued.

What is a widely accepted practice in our world today you have felt personally convicted is no longer okay for you?

I don't ask this to make us get more legalistic but rather honest. Wouldn't it be amazing to walk away from this study markedly different? To know that, because we did this study, we finally listened to and heeded a conviction we'd previously brushed off or ignored? I would imagine that you, like me, have something coming to mind that, if you gave it up, would provide your mind and your heart with less negative influence.

There was a long season of my life where I knew I had to give up watching TV. It's not that what I was watching was necessarily bad but it was negatively influencing me with something I needed to change. I didn't want to give up TV and easily justified not doing so. But once I finally did this for a season, it broke my addiction to needing it. It gave space for God to quiet my heart and mind and more clearly hear from Him. It made space for Bible study, relationships that needed my attention, and some inner healing I needed to attend to. The difficulty of giving it up on the front end paled in comparison to the huge benefits I experienced on the back end. Again, I'm not wanting us to get legalistic here but honest.

What would you be willing to give up for at least a season of your life?

Not only were the high places an issue in Josiah's day but also the practice of worshiping graven images or idols. You may not worship a literal graven image today, but, as we've discussed throughout this study, we all have things in our lives that distract us, making it easier to trust in things other than God. Josiah "put away" those distractions. He cleaned house.

Some things need to be given up for a season and some things need to be put away for good. What in your life do you need to "put away" to better focus on the one true God? Let the truth of God's Word lead you here.

Putting away distractions is another example of Josiah demonstrating the repetitive theme of returning to the Lord in both hearing and doing.

Yesterday, we looked at our covenant relationship with God. Let's study this a little so we can better understand the old covenant and the new covenant. The old covenant (Ex. 19–24) was made between God and the Israelites. However, the old covenant was established in anticipation of the new covenant that would fulfill all the expectations of the old covenant and would expand to all people.

> Look up the following verses and use them to compare and contrast the old and new covenants.
>
> Hebrews 8:1-2;9:1
>
>
> Hebrews 9:28
>
>
> Hebrews 9:7,12,18,22
>
>
> Hebrews 10:16

The old covenant was utterly limited; the new covenant, through grace, is divinely definitive for those who repent of their sin and turn to Jesus as the true trustworthy King.

I know it can seem cumbersome to do this comparison and to take time to write all of this out for the question above, but here's why it's so important to us today: What the people thought they were longing for was a king. In actuality, they were longing for a Savior. We have that same longing in our lives. The people were laser-focused on a king, but we get laser-focused on and ultimately put our trust in what we think will save us:

• A better political leader;

• A best friend who's always there for us;

• A spouse to unconditionally love us;

- A boss who has our future best interest in mind;
- A defender of our rights;
- A pastor who can be all things to all people.

Write down some of the people or things you can get laser-focused on to meet the deep longings of your heart.

It's not that we don't need to have expectations of these people in our lives. However, our expectations become unrealistic when we are misplacing our need for a divine Savior and wanting these people to become something they can never and should never be in our lives. Until we realize that what we're ultimately longing for is a Savior, all lesser solutions and lesser loves will disappoint and disillusion us.

Wow. All that we've discussed today is causing me to pause and really consider how to practically apply this to my heart and my life. Today's study is a little bit shorter so we can spend some extra time doing just that.

Reflect on the following questions as you end today's study.

What was your biggest personal takeaway from this week's study so far?

Where did you experience the most resistance to being challenged or convicted?

What are some things you could do to overcome this resistance?

How might your life be better and your relationship with the Lord closer if you continue to apply God's Word to your situation?

the TRUE KING

Think about how much we take for granted that our cell phones will work every day. But if we never recharge the battery, eventually the phone will lose its power. The phone is only as faithful as it is close to its real source of power. It may be okay on its own in the short term, but long term, without a power cord, the phone will become completely useless.

This begs us to ask, what is our source? What enables us to live with total trust, and how can we even be sure of this? John 1:1-3 teaches us the Source of all created things is Jesus. Nothing that has been made was made without Him. In Colossians 1:17 the apostle Paul wrote, "[Jesus] is before all things, and in him all things hold together." Jesus holds together creation, keeping it from falling into total chaos.

Jesus is the answer to our longing for stability, security, and a trustworthy authority that no earthly king can ever be.

Even Josiah, who followed the Lord and upheld His Law, couldn't escape the realities of his own humanity.

> Read 2 Chronicles 35:20-22, paying attention to the word *nevertheless* or *however*. Why is this word important here?

It might be strange for us to see this message coming from Josiah's enemy, but what a great reminder to us to always confirm something by going back to the Lord's Word for ourselves. And pay attention to what Josiah did next—he disguised himself. An act of hiding is an act of deceit and disobedience which ultimately revealed his lack of trust.

What was the result? How did Josiah's story end (2 Chron. 35:23-24)?

How might this same kind of resistance to seeking the Lord first get us in trouble as well?

Again, Jesus is the answer—He is the only way—and the only King who will never fall short. All other human substitutes will disappoint. For they themselves were longing for the king they could never be. After all, an earthly king could never be the same as the eternal King and Savior.

Each of the kings during our study was found to be in a place of longing and wanting, searching for a source of security and safety. All they needed to do was wholeheartedly turn to God, who was their King. Failing to do so caused serious trust issues for them and the people they were entrusted to lead. In fact, all of the kings we have studied have one glaring thing in common: They all fell short of the mark. We started our study talking about how the people of God wanted a king based on their observation of the nations around them.

> Let's take a moment to revisit Deuteronomy 17:14-20 and see which, if any, kings we studied kept each of the commands.

JESUS IS THE ANSWER TO OUR LONGING FOR STABILITY, SECURITY, AND A TRUSTWORTHY AUTHORITY THAT NO EARTHLY KING CAN EVER BE.

COMMANDS	SAUL	DAVID	SOLOMON	REHOBOAM	JEROBOAM	AHAB	JEHOASH	HEZEKIAH	JOSIAH
One from among your brothers	X	X	X	X	X	X	X	X	X
He shall not aquire many horses and he shall not acquire excessive silver and gold.									
He shall not cause the people to return to Egypt.	X	X	X	X	X	X	X	X	X
He shall not acquire many wives.					X	X	X	X	
He shall write for himself a copy of this law, he shall read in it all the days of his life, and he shall keep all the words of the law.									
His heart may not be lifted up above his brothers.		X					X		X
He may not turn aside from the commandment.									

Sobering, isn't it? None of these kings followed the Lord's commands. They didn't refrain from acquiring excessive possessions. They didn't write a copy of the law for themselves and then read it daily so they would not turn aside from God's commandments. Our study of these ancient kings keeps bringing us back to the only

One worthy of complete and total trust. What these earthly kings could not do, God made a way through His very own Son. Jesus condescended from the perfection of heaven into the chaos of the earth in the most unlikely manner. This word, *condescend*, in a biblical sense, indicates that something significant was laid down in order for a greater good to be achieved.

Jesus fulfills every aspect of the ideal king in Deuteronomy 17:14-20 and more. Now, let's examine each part of Jesus' fulfillment of these verses.

VERSE: "You may indeed set a king over you whom the Lord your God will choose" (Deut. 17:15a).

FULFILLMENT: GOD HIMSELF CHOSE JESUS as the only way for ultimate atonement to take place. The anticipation of Jesus is found all the way back in Genesis 3:15. The seed of the woman would conquer the seed of the serpent. This promise is fulfilled in Jesus.

Look up and summarize the following verses that also point to this truth: Romans 16:20

Galatians 3:16,19,29

VERSE: "One from among your brothers you shall set as king over you" (Deut. 17:15b).

FULFILLMENT: JESUS ENTERING INTO HUMANITY made atonement possible. Jesus took on humanity while preserving His total divinity in order to be like us humans in every way, yet without sin. Jesus becoming flesh Himself connected Him to the tribe of Judah through human blood—the very blood He shed to connect us through atonement to a redeemed relationship with God. And He is a merciful and faithful High Priest, who understands the true depth of human emotion, the complexity of human relationships, and the hardship of facing temptation.

Read Hebrews 2:14-18 and write out verse 17 below.

VERSE: "Only he must not acquire many horses for himself or cause the people to return to Egypt in order to acquire many horses, since the Lord has said to you, 'You shall never return that way again.' And he shall not acquire many wives for himself, lest his heart turn away, nor shall he acquire for himself excessive silver and gold" (Deut. 17:16-17).

FULFILLMENT: THE VERY NATURE OF THE BIRTH OF JESUS and the humility associated with it is astounding. God the Father could have chosen for His Son any situation and circumstance. Jesus could have been born in a palace (maybe this was even expected). Jesus could have been born to a wealthy family with means and opportunity. However, Jesus was born in a manger into a working-class family.

Look up and summarize the following verses that also point to this truth: Matthew 2:1-6; 8:20

Philippians 2:7

VERSE: "And when he sits on the throne of his kingdom, he shall write for himself in a book a copy of this law, approved by the Levitical priests. And it shall be with him, and he shall read in it all the days of his life, that he may learn to fear the Lord his God by keeping all the words of this law and these statutes, and doing them, that his heart may not be lifted up above his brothers, and that he may not turn aside from the commandment, either to the right hand or to the left" (Deut. 17:18-20).

FULFILLMENT: JESUS NOT ONLY KEPT THE STATUTES and law of God, He is the very Word of God (John 1:1,14).

Look up and summarize the following verses that also point to this truth: Mark 14:32-36

Luke 2:46-47

John 1:1,14

What my heart needs and what I want sometimes come into conflict with each other, much like with the children of Israel. What they needed was an eternal King who would provide deliverance through eternal salvation. What they wanted was an earthly king like the nations around them. However, the earthly kings would only provide temporary solutions and create more problems than they'd solve. They couldn't see what we now see in the historical context of these Scriptures. Therefore, they didn't heed the warning God gave them. I wish they had made the choice to trust Him, even when they couldn't see the detriments of a human king, so they could have better managed their desires. But what wasn't chosen by them—a full trust in God and a turning away from desires outside of God's best—is possible for us.

Let's learn the lessons unpacked through these important books of the Bible. Let's pray this prayer to close out the study:

Lord, help us to know how to apply these lessons to our lives today. Help us to see what we need to see, heed what we need to heed, and trust You, Lord, on a much greater level. You have no need to prove Your trustworthiness, and yet time and again we see You revealing how very faithful You are. I proclaim on this day, You are faithful. You are worthy of my trust. You are the trustworthy One I need to daily turn to and return to with all my desires, issues, fears, hard situations, relationship struggles, uncertainties, disappointments, disillusionments, and everything in between. You are the answer to my questions. You are the solution to my longings. You are the way when there seems to be no other way. You lead me, guide me, protect me, and save me. You are my Lord. You are my King. Amen and amen.

JESUS, THE GREATER ADAM: KING, PROPHET, PRIEST

Every move of God is a move of intention. When God created Adam and Eve, He created them with a purpose. God's purpose for Adam and Eve was to be fruitful and multiply, keep the garden, rule the creatures, and subdue the creation. If we drill down to the function of Adam, we could say that Adam was created to serve as prophet, priest, and king.

KING: God's intentional creation of Adam and Eve in His likeness and image (Gen. 1:26–27; 5:3) sets the stage for a kingly role in relationship to creation.[63]

> The LORD kills and brings to life; he brings down to Sheol and raises up. The LORD makes poor and makes rich; he brings low and he exalts. He raises up the poor from the dust; he lifts the needy from the ash heap to make them sit with princes and inherit a seat of honor. For the pillars of the earth are the LORD's, and on them he has set the world.
>
> 1 SAMUEL 2:6-8

Thinking about this passage above, especially God raising up the poor from the dust to seat them with princes, consider the way Adam came to life. Adam was given the breath of life directly from God (Gen. 2:7). Think about this. Adam was elevated from dust to being a human created in the image of God. A king is elevated from being a common man to a ruler over a kingdom.

Benjamin Gadd, quoting Walter Brueggemann, makes a connection with the dust imagery by contending "that the motif of elevation from 'dust' stems from a well-known royal tradition (cf. 1 Sam 2:6–8; 1 Kgs 16:2–3; Ps 113:7). [Brueggemann] claims, 'Adam, in Gen 2, is really being crowned king over the garden with all the power and authority which it implies' (12). If this is the case, which appears likely, then Adam created in God's image to rule over the earth in 1:26–28 is very similar to God elevating him to kingship in 2:7."[64]

PROPHET: Adam is also a type of prophet. God established Adam as His prophet in at least two ways: First, by rightly naming all of the animals (Gen. 2:19-20a); and second, by rightly describing his bride.[65]

PRIEST: Adam served as a type of priest because he was commanded to "keep" the garden (Gen. 2:15). The Hebrew word **šāmar** can also be translated as "guard" or "protect" and is the same word used of the priestly responsibilities given to the Levites.[66]

However, after the fall we find that what was once intentionally unified (the roles of prophet, priest, and king) became separated. With Moses we find a prophet and his brother Aaron a priest. With Saul we find a king, and it was not appropriate for a king to function or perform the duties of priest. Saul neglected and disobeyed this command and ultimately lost his kingdom.

Yet all was not lost. God's plan, delayed by sin, would not be defeated by sin. Rather, the divine Son of God would overcome sin and death. In Christ we find the fulfillment of the perfection of prophet, priest, and king. Christ is the perfect Prophet who declared the Word to humanity and called people to repentance through His own divine blood. Christ is the perfect High Priest who offered the ultimate sacrifice for sin, making restoration to the Father possible for those who repent of their sin and submit themselves to the kingship of Jesus. Christ is the one true King of heaven who reigns forever in perfect righteousness over all creation.

VIDEO SESSION 6: JOSIAH

WATCH VIDEO SESSION 6 AND RECORD YOUR NOTES BELOW.

_____

_____

_____

_____

_____

_____

_____

_____

_____

_____

_____

_____

_____

_____

_____

_____

_____

_____

_____

_____

_____

_____

_____

_____

_____

_____

_____

_____

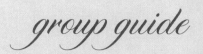

VIDEO GROUP DISCUSSION QUESTIONS

After watching the video, discuss the following questions in your group.

- Lysa referred to three things that demanding a human king resulted in. Talk about these things and how you were impacted by the visual of the temple being in ruins today.

- The ruins we saw in today's video are not the end of the story. What is Jesus' beautiful message of hope for us?

- What do you think or feel as you hear the statement, "No human authority is over God's authority ever"?

- What is a marked moment you've had during these last five weeks?

- What has this study revealed about where you've placed your trust?

- What is something new you've learned about the trustworthiness of God?

To access the video teaching sessions, use the instructions in the back of your Bible study book.

199

Leader Guide

Thank you for leading a group through *Trustworthy*. I so appreciate your willingness to share of yourself and help other women dig into God's Word. I hope that this Leader Guide helps you as you study together.

Each week you'll show a video teaching. You'll find detailed information on how to access the videos on the card inserted in the back of the Bible study book. If your group doesn't have adequate Internet connection for video streaming, DVD sets are available for purchase at *lifeway.com/trustworthy*. That is where you will also find promotional tools and other helpful resources.

You will find Group Guide pages for each session throughout the study. The Group Guide pages include room for notes to respond to the video teaching as well as discussion questions a group can talk through following the video.

In the back pages of this book, you'll find ten perforated cards, two for each week of personal study, with a quote and a question to help you process what you're learning. Encourage your group to tear those out, jot down a few notes on what they've studied or a prayer to help them live in trust, and place the cards where they'll see them often as a reminder of the One who is trustworthy above all.

The basic outline of each group session will be:

1. Discuss your personal study time from the past week. This Leader Guide will point you to specific questions from the week to look back on and answer together with your group.

2. Watch the video and take notes on what you hear.

3. Discuss the group questions on the Group Guide page.

4. Pray and dismiss.

For a study like this, the ideal time for your group is one hour. If you can meet longer, great, but you probably need at least an hour in order to have both good discussion and time to watch the videos.

Tips on Leading:

1. PRAY. As you prepare, remember that prayer is essential. Set aside time each week to pray for the women in your group. Listen to their needs and struggles so you can bring them before the Lord.

2. GUIDE. Accept women where they are but also set expectations that motivate commitment. Be consistent and trustworthy. Encourage women to follow through on the study, attend the group sessions, and engage in the personal study throughout the week. Listen carefully, responsibly guide discussion, and keep confidences shared within the group. Be honest and vulnerable by sharing what God is teaching you through the study. Most women will follow your lead if you share in a vulnerable way.

3. CONNECT. Stay engaged with the women. Use social media, email groups, or a quick note in the mail to connect with the group and share prayer needs throughout the week.

Tips on Organizing:

1. Talk to your pastor or minister over discipleship. If you're leading this as a part of a local church, ask for their input, prayers, and support.

2. Secure your location. Think about the number of women you can accommodate in the designated location. Reserve any tables, chairs, or media equipment for the videos that you may need.

3. Provide resources. Order the needed number of Bible study books for your group, or direct group members on how to order their own books. You might need to get a few extras for last minute additions.

4. Plan and prepare. Become familiar with the study and make notes of what information you need to share with your particular group.

Use the first session to build fellowship within your group. Familiarize yourself with the content of the study. Preview the study for the members so they will know what is expected each week.

1. Be sure each woman has a copy of the *Trustworthy* Bible study book.

2. Invite the women to introduce and share something about themselves.

3. Ask what drew each member to this study.

4. Without looking anything up, have the women talk about what they know of the biblical kings. It's okay if the answer is "not much!"

5. Ask why the women think we have these stories of the kings in the Bible.

6. Ask each woman to share what she hopes to learn and gain from this study. Jot their answers down to revisit later!

7. The women don't have to answer this out loud, but before you start the video for this week ask them to silently think of a time when they doubted God. Maybe they doubted His existence altogether or perhaps it was a characteristic of God—His goodness, His wisdom, His mercy, etc. (Again, this is the first group meeting—your group might want to discuss this, especially if you all know each other well. But if not, at least have them think about and write some thoughts down on the notes page. Having this information front and center in their heads will help prepare them for the video.)

8. Watch Video Session 1: *Introduction* and discuss the questions in the Group Guide (p. 11).

9. Review any information from the About This Study page (p. 8) you think women may need to know.

10. Instruct the participants to complete Week 1 of their personal study this week and come ready to discuss it at the next group meeting.

11. Pray and dismiss.

SESSION 2

1.   Questions to ask your group:

   a. *What was the most meaningful moment for you this week? It may be a Bible verse, principle, revelation, new understanding, or conviction.*

   b. *Read 1 Samuel 12:16-19 together. What was the weight of the want of a king for the people of Israel?*

   c. *Which one of the attributes of God on page 26 speaks most deeply to your heart right now? Why?*

   d. *How does David's story of sin and repentance give you hope for your story?*

   e. *Why do you think Solomon asked for wisdom? And how does his request highlight his trust in God at that point in his life?*

   f. *What does it practically look like to be a city on a hill? Who inspires you to be this way?*

   g. *Why do you think David was still called a man after God's own heart while Solomon was labeled differently?*

2.   Watch Video Session 2: *Solomon* and discuss the questions in the Group Guide (p. 51).

3.   Pray and dismiss.

SESSION 3

1.   Questions to ask your group:

   a. *What was the most meaningful moment for you this week? It may be a Bible verse, principle, revelation, new understanding, or conviction.*

   b. *Read 1 Kings 11:29-39 together. Now turn to 1 Samuel 15:24-29. What did Samuel prophesy to Saul? What symbol is used? What do these echoes from previous stories in Scripture teach us about God?*

       c. Have you ever feared losing the affection and respect of someone, whether in a friendship, a parenting relationship, a romantic relationship, or a working relationship? How did you react to your fear?

       d. Who do you go to for counsel now? Why do you go to that particular person or group of people?

       e. Why is the practice of remembering crucial in obedience to God?

       f. Why is the justice of God a good thing?

2. Watch Video Session 3: *Jeroboam* and discuss the questions in the Group Guide (p. 89).

3. Pray and dismiss.

SESSION 4

1. Questions to ask your group:

       a. What was the most meaningful moment for you this week? It may be a Bible verse, principle, revelation, new understanding, or conviction.

       b. How have you seen God lovingly call someone to turn from his or her self-reliance leading to sin and return to Him? How have you seen Him remind you to turn your heart back to Him?

       c. When have you seen God provide both a want and a need, perhaps in your life or in the life of someone you know?

       d. Has there been a situation in your life where you've attempted to "take possession"? What did your reaction to the situation reveal about your heart?

       e. In Day 4, we discussed everyone in Jehoash's story doing their part to begin to restore the temple. How has someone doing his or her part made an impact on your life and walk with Christ?

       f. Do you find it easier to trust God with your actions or your devotion?

2. Watch Video Session 4: *Ahab* and discuss the questions in the Group Guide (p. 123).

3. Pray and dismiss.

SESSION 5

1. Questions to ask your group:

   a. *What was the most meaningful moment for you this week? It may be a Bible verse, principle, revelation, new understanding, or conviction.*

   b. *What do you think it means when God commanded His people to be fruitful and multiply?*

   c. *What is one thing you've learned about trusting God that you've found helpful in your harder circumstances?*

   d. *Describe a circumstance in your life in which you longed for a rescuer. Who or what did you turn to at that time for rescue or deliverance?*

   e. *How do you think the word* return *might speak to God's faithfulness? Think of stories in the Bible where a similar term might be used.*

   f. *How is God asking you to trust Him today?*

2. Watch Video Session 5: *Hezekiah* and discuss the questions in the Group Guide (p. 159).

3. Pray and dismiss.

SESSION 6

This is your last week together with your group. Congratulate your group on sticking with this study and praise their efforts for getting into the Word of God together. Challenge them to teach/lead others—either through leading this study with another person or group or simply by sharing some of the truths they've learned with those in their sphere of influence.

1. Questions to ask your group:

    a. *What was the most meaningful moment for you this week? It may be a Bible verse, principle, revelation, new understanding, or conviction.*

    b. *What are some ways you can be saturated in God's Word in your everyday? Try thinking outside the box of simply reading the Bible (though that is important too).*

    c. *What does it mean to revere? Look up the word in a dictionary or online if you need to and then write the definition in your own words. How did Josiah's seeking God demonstrate his reverence of Him?*

    d. *Josiah heard, he inquired, he received the message, and then he responded both personally and publicly. Does this progression speak to the way we react when we hear God's Word taught today? Share your thoughts with the group.*

    e. *What in your life do you need to "put away" to better focus on the one true God?*

2. Watch Video Session 6: *Josiah* and discuss the questions in the Group Guide (p. 199).

3. Pray and dismiss.

Guide to 1 & 2 Kings

If you're curious about the rest of the story, here's where you can find out more about each of the kings in 1 & 2 Kings!

Solomon
1 Kings 1–11

Rehoboam
1 Kings 12; 14

Jeroboam I
1 Kings 12–14

Abijah
1 Kings 15

Asa
1 Kings 15

Nadab
1 Kings 15

Baasha
1 Kings 16

Elah
1 Kings 16

Zimri
1 Kings 16

Omri
1 Kings 16

Ahab
1 Kings 17–21

Ahaziah
1 Kings 22;
2 Kings 1–2

Joram
2 Kings 3–7

Jehoram
2 Kings 8

Ahaziah
2 Kings 8–9

Jehu
2 Kings 9–10

Athaliah
2 Kings 11

Jehoash
2 Kings 11–12

Jehoahaz
2 Kings 13

Jehoash
2 Kings 13–14

Jeroboam II
2 Kings 14

Amaziah
2 Kings 14

Uzziah
2 Kings 15

Jotham
2 Kings 15

Zechariah
2 Kings 15

Shallum
2 Kings 15

Menahem
2 Kings 15

Pekahiah
2 Kings 15

Pekah
2 Kings 15

Ahaz
2 Kings 16

Hoshea
2 Kings 17

Hezekiah
2 Kings 18–20

Manasseh
2 Kings 21

Amon
2 Kings 21

Josiah
2 Kings 22–23

Jehoahaz
2 Kings 23

Jehoiakim
2 Kings 23–24

Jehoiachin
2 Kings 24–25

Zedekiah
2 Kings 24–25

10 STATEMENTS OF TRUTH
TO DECLARE YOUR TRUST IN GOD

BY LYSA TERKEURST

When God's Word is spoken into our situations and circumstances, **truth** lays the foundation for **trust** to be built. For those of you, like me, who need to take back territory in places distrust has settled in, here are ten scriptural statements we can speak over our lives. When we declare God's truth, doubt decreases, fear flees, and skepticism ceases to hold us captive.

TODAY, I DECLARE DOUBT MUST FLEE BECAUSE I CAN TRUST YOU AT ALL TIMES.

"Trust in him at all times, O people;
pour out your heart before him;
God is a refuge for us. Selah"
(Psalm 62:8)

Whether my faith feels strong today or not, I can trust God at all times. God, whether I can see or I feel utterly in the dark, I can honestly come to You about the places and situations where I keep finding myself living in doubt. God, I know that You are a refuge for me in every place and situation. Help grow my faith in places I'm doubting Your promises, Your provision, or Your presence.

TODAY, I DECLARE DOUBT MUST FLEE BECAUSE THE LORD ALONE IS MY TRUST.

"Blessed is the man who makes
the LORD his trust,
who does not turn to the proud,
to those who go astray after a lie!"
(Psalm 40:4)

When I find myself faced with uncertainty, I am tempted to run to things other than You, God. I know that You oppose the proud but give grace to the humble. So today, I ask for Your grace as I practice running straight to You in humility, rather than running away from You in fear. When I am triggered by something and tempted to pull away, I pray I remember the safety and comfort found in Your embrace every single time I choose to run to You.

TODAY, I DECLARE DOUBT MUST FLEE BECAUSE I'M SHIFTING FROM SELF-SUFFICIENCY TO SACRIFICE, PUTTING TRUST BACK IN GOD'S HANDS.

"Offer right sacrifices,
and put your trust in the LORD."
(Psalm 4:5)

"I appeal to you therefore, brothers, by the mercies of God, to present your bodies
as a living sacrifice, holy and acceptable to God, which is your spiritual worship."
(Romans 12:1)

From the time I wake up in the morning until it's time for me to go to sleep, I know there are things begging for my attention other than You, God. The weight of my problem begs me to give in to self-made solutions that leave no room for You to move. I pray today would not be a day of self-sufficiency, but a day of self-sacrifice. I offer myself to You as a living sacrifice because I know You are worthy of my trust.

TODAY, I DECLARE DOUBT MUST FLEE BECAUSE I AM TRUSTING IN YOUR STEADFAST LOVE FOR ME, KNOWING YOU'VE DONE IT BEFORE AND YOU CAN DO IT AGAIN.

"'See the man who would not make
God his refuge,
but trusted in the abundance of his riches
and sought refuge in his own destruction!'
But I am like a green olive tree
in the house of God.
I trust in the steadfast love of God
forever and ever.
I will thank you forever,
because you have done it.
I will wait for your name, for it is good,
in the presence of the godly."
(Psalm 52:7–9)

God, I confess that sometimes I forget to remember Your faithfulness from the past, especially when I am overwhelmed with unpredictable things in front of me today. Bring to my mind that Your steadfast love for me helps me know with confidence You are a safe place for me to process my doubts and fears. I don't know exactly what tomorrow will look like, but I do know who I'll be looking to—You, Lord—whose love is unfailing and whose hand is the safest place to entrust my hope.

TODAY, I DECLARE DOUBT MUST FLEE AS I TRANSFER PUTTING MY ULTIMATE TRUST IN PEOPLE TO TRUSTING THE GOD WHO HEARS ME.

"Put no trust in a neighbor;
have no confidence in a friend;
guard the doors of your mouth
from her who lies in your arms;
for the son treats the father with contempt,
the daughter rises up against her mother,
the daughter-in-law against her mother-in-law;
a man's enemies are the men of his own house.
But as for me, I will look to the Lord;
I will wait for the God of my salvation;
my God will hear me."
(Micah 7:5–7)

It is so easy for me to carry the wounds of my past and present hurts from friends or family into my relationship with You, God. I pray for forgiveness toward any past hurt I am still wrestling through, any words that still sting with pain, or any relationship that feels like it will never get better. God, I look to You to be the only source of unwavering trust in my life. Help strengthen my heart when it becomes weary from seasons of waiting, and when relationships don't get better. I know that You hear my cries and prayers. Help me keep my eyes fixed on You and You alone, knowing humans may be imperfect, but You are perfect and present in every season. When I am discouraged about the way relationships are going in my life, help me turn those feelings into an opportunity to build even more trust in my relationship with You. I know You see me and are for me.

 TODAY, I DECLARE DOUBT MUST FLEE BECAUSE I AM PLANTED FIRMLY IN GOD'S FAITHFULNESS.

"Thus says the Lord:
'Cursed is the man who trusts in man
and makes flesh his strength,
whose heart turns away from the Lord.
He is like a shrub in the desert,
and shall not see any good come.
He shall dwell in the parched places of the wilderness,
in an uninhabited salt land.
'Blessed is the man who trusts in the Lord,
whose trust is the Lord.
He is like a tree planted by water,
that sends out its roots by the stream,
and does not fear when heat comes,
for its leaves remain green,
and is not anxious in the year of drought,
for it does not cease to bear fruit.'"
(Jeremiah 17:5-8)

God, I am so tempted to isolate myself even from You when fear arises. Help me break the pattern of turning away from You and replace it with turning straight to You. Today, I declare that I will not be shaken when trouble comes, but I will be strengthened. Through every season, good and difficult, help me turn away from fear and anxiousness and, instead, grow in trust. Help me learn how to bear fruit in every season, not wavering, even through storms that come, You are the Master over it all.

TODAY, I DECLARE DOUBT MUST FLEE BECAUSE GOD'S WORD ALWAYS PROVES TRUE.

"Every word of God proves true;
he is a shield to those who take refuge in him."
(Proverbs 30:5)

God, if I'm being honest, sometimes I shrink back in fear and doubt when I read Your Word because there are places in my heart not trusting that Your promises are true for me. I know Your Word has the ultimate authority, but I find myself quick to forget it's true for me too. Today, I choose to believe in the truth of Your Word entirely. I am choosing to look at You before I look at my circumstances. I know You are always faithful. Help me make Your Word the shield that I hold up and your truth the comfort I cling to in refuge.

TODAY, I DECLARE DOUBT MUST FLEE BECAUSE GOD IS MY RESCUE.

"He trusts in the LORD; let him deliver him;
let him rescue him, for he delights in him!"
(Psalm 22:8)

God, at times I feel like my fear is swallowing me whole. I find myself in a deep pit of despair without hope. I am in need of rescue from the lies I believe and the doubt that creeps in. Today, I declare that You are my rescue, for you delight in me, and You will deliver me from my unbelief.

TODAY, I DECLARE DOUBT MUST FLEE BECAUSE GOD IS A STRONGHOLD.

"The LORD is a stronghold for the oppressed,
a stronghold in times of trouble.
And those who know your name put their trust in you,
for you, O LORD, have not forsaken those who seek you."
(Psalm 9:9-10)

I confess that when I'm at the end of my rope, I am more prone to turn away from trusting You. Thank You for being a stronghold for me when I am overwhelmed. I pray that my heart would be drawn to seek You first when I feel oppressed. Your name alone brings power and authority to places doubt has crept in. I praise You in advance that when I seek You, You will never forsake me.

TODAY I DECLARE DOUBT MUST FLEE BECAUSE EVEN WHEN THINGS FEEL OUT OF CONTROL, GOD IS IN CONTROL.

"Let every person be subject to the governing authorities.
For there is no authority except from God, and those that exist have been instituted by God."
(Romans 13:1)

Lord, it is easy for me to become troubled at the injustice and turmoil in the world. I confess that sometimes it is difficult for me to trust You are in control when circumstances around me feel out of control. God, help me humble myself even when I don't understand, knowing that there is nothing out of Your sight or control. Today, I pray for those in leadership over me, both in our country and in the world. Rather than staying fixated on the things going on in our physical world, I pray that I would be focused on seeing You in the midst of it all.

ENDNOTES

1. Wayne A. Grudem, *Systematic Theology: An Introduction to Biblical Doctrine* (Leicester, England; Grand Rapids, MI: InterVarsity Press; Zondervan, 2004).

2. *Ibid.*

3. C. S. Lewis, *Words to Live by: A Guide for the Merely Christian*, ed. Paul F. Ford, Adobe Digital Edition (HarperCollins e-books, 2009), 291.

4. Louis Berkhof, *Systematic Theology* (Grand Rapids, MI: Wm. B. Eerdmans Publishing, 1938), 69.

5. Grudem.

6. Brandon Grafius, "Solomon, King of Israel," ed. John D. Barry et al., *The Lexham Bible Dictionary* (Bellingham, WA: Lexham Press, 2016).

7. Strong's; *https://www.blueletterbible.org/kjv/1ki/8/1/ss1/s_299001.*

8. Strong's H2617; *https://www.blueletterbible.org/lang/Lexicon/Lexicon.cfm?strongs=H2617&t=KJV.*

9. Taken from Lysa TerKeurst's teaching on Proverbs 31 Ministries' First 5 app; *https://first5.org/plans/1-2%20kings/ff_kings_12/.*

10. Adapted from John T. Swann, "High Place," ed. John D. Barry et al., *The Lexham Bible Dictionary* (Bellingham, WA: Lexham Press, 2016).

11. Strong's "Trustworthy"; *https://www.blueletterbible.org/search/search. cfm?Criteria=trustworthy&t=ESV#s=s_primary_0_1.*

12. Strong's H982; *https://www.blueletterbible.org/lang/Lexicon/Lexicon.cfm?strongs=H982&t=KJV.*

13. Strong's G4103; *https://www.blueletterbible.org/lang/Lexicon/Lexicon.cfm?strongs=G4103&t=KJV.*

14. Strong's "Trustworthy"; *https://www.blueletterbible.org/search/search. cfm?Criteria=trustworthy&t=ESV#s=s_primary_0_1.*

15. Information found in the Connecting the Kings summary was taken from Bible Gateway; *https://www.biblegateway.com/blog/2017/07/updated-chart-of-israels-and-judahs-kings-and-prophets/.*

16. Carl Friedrich Keil and Franz Delitzsch, *Commentary on the Old Testament*, vol. 3 (Peabody, MA: Hendrickson, 1996), 124.

17. C. H. Spurgeon, "'This Thing Is from Me,'" in *The Metropolitan Tabernacle Pulpit Sermons*, vol. 42 (London: Passmore & Alabaster, 1896), 363.

18. Paul House, *1, 2 Kings,* The New American Commentary, vol. 8 (Nashville, TN: Broadman & Holman Publishers, 2011).

19. Geoffrey W. Bromiley, "Doubt" in *The International Standard Bible Encyclopedia, A-D* (Grand Rapids, MI: William. B. Eerdmans Publishing Company, 1979), 987.

20. Charles Draper, Archie England, and Chad Brand, eds., *Holman Illustrated Bible Dictionary* (Nashville, TN: Holman Bible Publishers, 2003) 1336.

22. House.

22. Information found in the Connecting the Kings summary was taken from Bible Gateway; *https://www.biblegateway.com/blog/2017/07/updated-chart-of-israels-and-judahs-kings-and-prophets/.*

23. Draper, England, and Brand, eds., 37.

24. *Ibid.*, 293.

25. *Ibid.*, 37.

26. Gary Staats, *1 & 2 Kings*, Old Testament Commentary (Portland, OR: Western Conservative Baptist Seminary, 1977), 127.

27. Leslie C. Allen, *Ezekiel 20–48*, Word Biblical Commentary (Dallas, TX: Word, Inc., 1998), 38.

28. James Swanson, *Dictionary of Biblical Languages with Semantic Domains: Hebrew (Old Testament)* (Oak Harbor: Logos Research Systems, Inc., 1997).

29. Strong's H5588; *https://www.blueletterbible.org/lang/Lexicon/Lexicon.cfm?strongs=H5588&t=KJV.*

30. Strong's H3423; *https://www.blueletterbible.org/lang/Lexicon/Lexicon. cfm?page=3&strongs=H3423&t=KJV#lexResults.*

31. Proverbs 31 Ministries, *Proverbs: The Beginning of all Wisdom,* The First 5 App Experience Guide (Matthews, NC: Proverbs 31 Ministries, 2018), 10.

32. T. Desmond Alexander, *From Eden to the New Jerusalem: An Introduction to Biblical Theology* (Grand Rapids: Kregel Academic & Professional, 2009), 82.

33. Swanson.

34. Wiseman, 251.

35. Brandon Ridley, "Jehoshaphat, King of Judah," ed. John D. Barry et al., The Lexham Bible Dictionary (Bellingham, WA: Lexham Press, 2016).

36. Swanson.

37. *Ibid.*

38. Information found in the Connecting the Kings summary was taken from Bible Gateway; *https:// www.biblegateway.com/blog/2017/07 updated-chart-of-israels-and-judahs-kings-and-prophets/.*

39. Lysa TerKeurst, *It's Not Supposed to Be This Way* (Nashville, TN: Thomas Nelson, 2018), 23.

40. Alexander.

41. Strong's H982; *https://www.blueletterbible.org/lang/Lexicon/Lexicon.cfm?strongs=H982&t=KJV.*

42. Taken from Lysa TerKeurst's First 5 app; *https://first5.org/plans/1-2%20Kings/ff_kings_30/.*

43. House.

44. Jesse C. Long, "1 & 2 Kings" in *College Press NIV Commentary* (Joplin, MO: College Press, 2002), 476.

45. Taken from Lysa TerKeurst's devotional; *https://proverbs31.org/read/devotions/ full-post/2016/09/22/why-you-dont-have-to-fear-the-upcoming-election.*

46. Strong's H5337; *https://www.blueletterbible.org/lang/Lexicon/Lexicon. cfm?strongs=H5337&t=KJV&ss=1.*

47. *Ibid.*

48. Long, 479.

49. Strong's H5599; *https://www.blueletterbible.org/lang/Lexicon/Lexicon.cfm?strongs=H5599&t=KJV.*

50. Donald J. Wiseman, *1 and 2 Kings,* Tyndale Old Testament Commentaries (Downers Grove, IL: InterVarsity Press, 1993), 302.

51. Long, 479

52. House.

53. T. R. Hobbs, *2 Kings,* Word Biblical Commentary (Dallas, TX: Word, Inc., 1995), 295.

54. G. K. Beale, *We Become What We Worship: A Biblical Theology of Idolatry* (Downers Grove, IL: IVP Academic, 2008), 64.

55. Information found in the Connecting the Kings summary was taken from Bible Gateway; *https://www.biblegateway.com/blog/2017/07/updated-chart-of-israels-and-judahs-kings-and-prophets/.*

56. Beale, 64.

57. Long, 505.

58. Draper, England, and Brand, eds., 1336.

59. Strong's H3665; *https://www.blueletterbible.org/lang/Lexicon/Lexicon.cfm?strongs=H3665&t=KJV.*

60. Carey C. Newman, "Covenant, New Covenant," *Dictionary of the Later New Testament and Its Developments* (Downers Grove, IL: InterVarsity Press, 1997), 245.

61. Kevin J. Vanhoozer, ed., *Dictionary for Theological Interpretation of the Bible* (Grand Rapids, MI: Baker Academic, 2004), 72.

62. William Lee Holladay, ed., *A Concise Hebrew and Aramaic Lexicon of the Old Testament* (Leiden, The Netherlands: E. J. Brill, 1988), 275.

63. Peter J. Link Jr. and Matthew Y. Emerson, "Searching for the Second Adam: Typological Connections between Adam, Joseph, Mordecai, and Daniel," *Southern Baptist Journal of Theology* 21, Spring 2017.

64. Walter Brueggemann, as quoted by Benjamin Gladd, *Revealing the Mysterion: The Use of Mystery in Daniel and Second Temple* (Berlin, Germany: Walter de Gruyte, 2008).

65. Link Jr. and Emerson.

66. G. K. Beale, *The Temple and the Church's Mission: A Biblical Theology of the Dwelling Place of God*, ed. D. A. Carson, New Studies in Biblical Theology (Downers Grove, IL; England: InterVarsity Press; Apollos, 2004), 81.

What is the deep cry of your heart?

That ache in your soul that keeps you up at night? The prayer you keep repeating? Jesus not only cares about this deep, spiritual wrestling, but He also wants to step in and see you through it.

Join Lysa TerKeurst on the streets of Israel to explore the seven I AM statements of Jesus found in the Gospel of John. Through this interactive, in-depth study, you will learn to:

• Trade feelings of emptiness and depletion for a more personal fulfillment from knowing who Jesus is.

• Stop living like a slave to your circumstances by training your heart to embrace the truth God wants to reveal to you.

• Gain a better understanding of how Jesus' words 2,000 years ago are so very applicable to the answers we are searching for today.

lifeway.com/findingiam | 800.458.2772

222   TRUSTWORTHY   Lifeway women

The free app you've been looking for!
Give God your first thoughts every day.

"We must exchange whispers with God before shouts with the world."

Lysa TerKeurst

We say we put God first... so wouldn't it make sense that we give Him the first 5 minutes of each day? That's why Proverbs 31 Ministries created the First 5 app.

- Honor God by letting His truth direct your first thoughts of the day and discover how much healthier your perspective of life becomes.
- Discover unique parts of the Bible you may have missed by studying one verse in one chapter, one day at a time.
- Replace feelings of comparison and rejection that social media often brings by starting your day with the truth of God's Word.
- Gain confidence in your ability to navigate Scripture by learning to identify the major moments in each chapter.

Download the app for FREE!

Download on the **App Store**

Get it on **Google play**

FIRST5.ORG

Get the most from your study.

COMPANION PRODUCTS

DVD Set, includes 6 video teaching sessions from Lysa TerKeurst, approximately 15–20 minutes each

IN THIS STUDY YOU'LL:

- Identify and challenge doubts in the one true God
- Explore how the Old Testament applies to our lives today
- Learn to trust in the goodness and faithfulness of God

To enrich your study experience, consider the accompanying *Trustworthy* video teaching sessions, approximately 15–20 minutes each, from Lysa TerKeurst.

STUDYING ON YOUR OWN?

Watch Lysa TerKeurst's teaching sessions, available via redemption code for individual video-streaming access, printed in this Bible study book.

LEADING A GROUP?

Each group member will need a *Trustworthy* Bible study book, which includes video access. Because all participants will have access to the video content, you can choose to watch the videos outside of your group meeting if desired. Or, if you're watching together and someone misses a group meeting, they'll have the flexibility to catch up! A DVD set is also available to purchase separately if desired.

Browse study formats, a free session sample, video clips, church promotional materials, and more at

lifeway.com/trustworthy

THERE IS A WEIGHT TO MY EVERY WANT.

LYSA TERKEURST, *TRUSTWORTHY*

WE DON'T HAVE TO UNDERSTAND THE WHY OF GOD'S WAYS. BUT WE DO HAVE TO KEEP CHOOSING TO FOLLOW THEM.

LYSA TERKEURST, *TRUSTWORTHY*

How can I rest in the peace God offers even in the midst of hard things?

_____
_____
_____
_____
_____
_____
_____
_____
_____
_____
_____
_____
_____
_____
_____

What is the biggest lesson I've learned this week in studying the lives of Saul, David, and Solomon?

_____
_____
_____
_____
_____
_____
_____
_____
_____
_____
_____

IF WE STRAY FROM GOD'S WORD, WE WILL STRAY FROM GOD HIMSELF.

LYSA TERKEURST, *TRUSTWORTHY*

WHATEVER CAPTIVATES OUR HEARTS FUELS OUR ACTIONS.

LYSA TERKEURST, *TRUSTWORTHY*

How can I keep myself rooted in God's Word during this season of life?

_____

_____

_____

_____

_____

_____

_____

_____

_____

_____

_____

What is the biggest lesson I've learned this week in studying the lives of Rehoboam and Jeroboam?

_____

_____

_____

_____

_____

_____

_____

_____

_____

_____

JUST BECAUSE WE DON'T ALWAYS SEE GOD'S ACTIVITY DOESN'T MEAN THERE IS A LACK OF ACTIVITY.

LYSA TERKEURST, *TRUSTWORTHY*

OUR ACTS OF OBEDIENCE ARE EVIDENCE OF OUR TRUST IN GOD.

LYSA TERKEURST, *TRUSTWORTHY*

How would my life and level of trust in God change if I lived according to this truth?

_____

_____

_____

_____

_____

_____

_____

_____

_____

_____

_____

_____

What is the biggest lesson I've learned this week in studying the lives of Ahab and Jehoash?

_____

_____

_____

_____

_____

_____

_____

_____

_____

_____

_____

_____

NOTHING TESTS OUR TRUST LIKE FEAR. BUT FEAR FADES WHEN WE TRUST THE STRENGTH AND SOVEREIGNTY OF OUR GOD.

LYSA TERKEURST, *TRUSTWORTHY*

THE BATTLE IS EITHER WON OR LOST BASED ON THE DECISIONS THAT FLOW FROM OUR MINDS.

LYSA TERKEURST, *TRUSTWORTHY*

How does this truth help me trust God more today?

_____
_____
_____
_____
_____
_____
_____
_____
_____
_____

What is the biggest lesson I've learned this week in studying the life of Hezekiah?

_____
_____
_____
_____
_____
_____
_____
_____
_____
_____
_____
_____

GOD ISN'T TRYING TO HIDE FROM US. HE IS WAITING TO BE SEEN BY US.

LYSA TERKEURST, *TRUSTWORTHY*

JESUS IS THE ANSWER TO OUR LONGING FOR STABILITY, SECURITY, AND A TRUSTWORTHY AUTHORITY THAT NO EARTHLY KING CAN EVER BE.

LYSA TERKEURST, *TRUSTWORTHY*

In what ways can I be intentional about seeing God in my everyday life?

_____
_____
_____
_____
_____
_____
_____
_____
_____
_____

What is the biggest lesson I've learned this week in studying the life of Josiah?

_____
_____
_____
_____
_____
_____
_____
_____
_____
_____
_____
_____
_____
_____

HERE'S YOUR VIDEO ACCESS.

To stream *Trustworthy* Bible study video teaching sessions, follow these steps:

1. Go to my.lifeway.com/redeem and register or log in to your Lifeway account.

2. Scratch off the foil below to reveal your redemption code. Enter this redemption code to gain access to your individual-use video license:

GCE449HQQW

Once you've entered your personal redemption code, you can stream the video teaching sessions any time from your Digital Media page on my.lifeway.com or watch them via the Lifeway On Demand app on any TV or mobile device via your Lifeway account.

There's no need to enter your code more than once! To watch your streaming videos, just log in to your Lifeway account at my.lifeway.com or watch using the Lifeway On Demand app.

QUESTIONS? WE HAVE ANSWERS!
Visit support.lifeway.com and search "Video Redemption Code" or call our Tech Support Team at 866.627.8553.

This video access code entitles you to one non-transferable, single-seat license with no expiration date. Please do not share your code with others. Videos are subject to expiration at the discretion of the publisher. Do not post Bible study videos to YouTube, Vimeo, any social media channel, or other online services for any purpose. Such posting constitutes copyright infringement and is prohibited by the terms of use. Unauthorized posting also violates the service rules, which can negatively affect your YouTube or other service account.